Building Trusting Relationships

The Complete Guide to Building and Nurturing Trust in Relationships

Mrs. Ashiya & Mr. Ashiya

Table of Contents

Table of Contents

Introduction

More than anything else, we all want to be happy. It is our basic drive. Everything we do—even if it's just working a job that has nothing to do with our interests—is to ensure some happiness for ourselves. That job will, at the very least, gain you some money, with which you could buy concert tickets, new clothes, or a nice meal.

But chances are, you won't attend those concerts, wear those clothes, or eat that delicious food alone. Unless you're a hermit of the olden times, content to live in a cave for years and years, the delights of life are shared. What greater happiness is there than having someone with which to dance to good music? Someone to admire your new outfit? Someone to steal fries from?

Much of our happiness and our fulfillment comes from our relationships with others. A fulfilling relationship can make any place feel less lonely: a new city, a new office, even a new apartment. Good emotional bonds with others can introduce you to entirely new interests or foster ones you already have. They can even help you achieve professional success, or support you through your darkest times.

Through our relationships, we understand other people, their worldviews, their interests, their wants and fears. We gain empathy and perspective, and often become richer ourselves for exploring others' minds and hearts. We become kinder so as to avoid causing pain in those we love. We try new things and go places we have never gone before.

So too, by developing bonds with others, we understand ourselves: how we are the same from others, and also how we are different. We also gain confidence simply by the act of being appreciated by someone else. What our friends love about us is what we learn to recognize in ourselves; the strengths our bosses see in our work affirm our own confidence in our abilities.

In short, relationships are what tie us to the world, and even to ourselves.

And what more do we want from life, and from our relationships, than security? The certainty that we are safe and loved, and will continue to be?

This book is about what happens when relationships fail to provide that security.

We must trust in our bonds with other people. To feel like we can depend on those whom we love. That we can not only share jokes and cheese boards with them, but that we can also tell them our worries, work on a team with them, even marry them, and never fear cruelty, abandonment, or betrayal.

But who among us has never, in our lives, been the subject of a cruel comment or joke? Who among us hasn't been ghosted by a date, or been purposefully cut loose by a friend? Who among us hasn't felt our insecurities mocked by someone we love, or been undercut so another could succeed? Or worse?

And who hasn't done all these things themselves, even if just once in their lives?

Relationships are bonds between two people—and people are fallible. We make mistakes, we act selfishly, and we hurt those we love most. This is an indisputable fact of life, and yet it is one of the most painful facts to face.

Especially when we, ourselves, have made such mistakes and broken others' trust in us.

It can feel easier, sometimes, to write off relationships that are bruised by wrongdoing. It's frightening to process our own hurt and to confront the one who hurt us. And it's terrifying to be confronted, to face our own guilt and shame for hurting another person. To open ourselves to criticism, or to ask someone to do better.

Often it feels impossible to even find the right words to do such a thing. And, if we found the right words, would we ever be brave enough to say them?

In this book, we argue: Yes.

Because we will give you the words. We will give you the tools. We will give you the confidence, and the belief that above all, you deserve to have relationships founded on trust, to feel happy, loved, and secure.

Having learned all this, you will see that bravery really has nothing to do with it.

First, of course, we must define the words 'relationship' and 'trust,' and analyze what those mean within different contexts. There are many different forms and characteristics that relationships and trust can take, and all of them require specific approaches if you want to strengthen them.

Then, we'll analyze how we ourselves approach relationships. Using attachment theory, we'll explore our gut reactions to intimacy and closeness, and how understanding more about how we individually process relationships can strengthen them altogether.

Then we'll move on to how to recognize signs of discontent, both physically and emotionally, and how to believe your own perceptions and intuitions. In short: if you feel like something is wrong, then something *is* wrong, and it is valid and necessary to address it.

Chapters 5, 6, and 7 discuss that most terrifying of prospects: betrayal. Someone else's, and our own. How to cope with feelings of betrayal or conversely feelings of shame and guilt. How to forgive and rebuild, or move on if rebuilding is impossible; and of course how to ask for forgiveness and begin the process of proving ourselves once more.

While the fifth and seventh chapters focus more broadly on betrayal, the sixth chapter will explore the effects of trauma on any relationship and discuss how to begin trusting again and build healthy relationships despite your past.

Everyone is entitled to respect, and because everyone is unique, so should the form that that respect takes.

When building a new relationship or strengthening an old one, we must be considerate of how we respect the other person, and feel comfortable asking for the respect that we need as well. In Chapter 8 we'll delve deep into boundaries: what they are, how they help, and how to follow them.

Chapter 9 covers the only thing more terrifying than betrayal: vulnerability. Why is it important to the success of a relationship? How can you move past the fear of vulnerability, especially after being burned one too many times? We'll answer all those questions and more, so vulnerability is something you desire and strive for, not something you avoid.

But how do you apply all these lessons to your real, personal relationships? In Chapter 10, we'll talk about how to approach your loved ones and check in on their feelings as well as your own. Even if there has been no big betrayal, sometimes trust erodes on its own, or it could be maintained in a better way; in this chapter we'll explore how to start those sometimes awkward, but always valuable conversations.

Last, but definitely not least, we explore our connections to and trust in ourselves. Our relationships with ourselves are the most important in our lives—the deepest and most certainly the longest. Why not go one step further, and make them the best and most dependable relationships we have?

To have truly successful and loving bonds with others, we must first and foremost have a successful and loving bond with ourselves. The lessons in these chapters do not just apply to our family, our friends, our partners; they apply to us, too.

Within these pages, you'll find all the tools to cultivate fulfilling, worthwhile relationships, not only with others but with yourself. To feel, most of all, that your bonds attest to your own goodness and that of those you love.

Because you are good, you are trustworthy, and you deserve to have people in your life whom you can depend on for anything, and whom you can love without restraint, doubt, or conditions.

Unfortunately, "trust issues" are some of the most common obstacles in our relationships today. And it's totally normal to feel that, after some hurts and betrayals, you can never again completely trust another person. Simply by living and loving, we are vulnerable to pain. All of us have experienced it. All of us even, to some extent, expect it.

But there is a difference between expecting pain and hurt as a normal side effect of life, and expecting the worst of people, or of ourselves, always.

In doing so, we only let ourselves down. Because we always see the world as we want to see it, choosing to see *only* untrustworthiness, deception, and disillusionment undoubtedly blinds us to all the goodness, honor, and love in the world. Our perceptions do shape our experiences, and so to help ourselves experience good things, we must believe good things are possible.

If nothing else, we must give others the chance to prove themselves. Over and over again, no matter how often we are disappointed. We must pick ourselves up, dust ourselves off, open the dialogue again, and try, try, try.

This requires work. It requires steadfast belief in your own worth and in the importance of love and trust in your life. It requires the willingness to forgive, the humility to apologize, and the bravery to open your heart again, even if it is bruised. It requires honest and consistent communication.

Everyone knows that creating and keeping good relationships is not as easy as just making a pinky promise to be good to each other; trust and happiness are flowers that need constant watering and tending to bloom. But here, in these pages, are the best methods of watering and tending.

Real trust and happiness are achievable, if only you are willing to put in the work.

Chapter 1:
What is a Relationship?

Of course, we all know the answer to that question. We all have relationships, formed simply by the fact of our existence: with our mothers, our fathers, our siblings. No one comes into this world alone. And chances are that, by going through life, you've gained— and perhaps lost—other relationships, such as childhood friends, romantic sweethearts, or influential teachers. Later, perhaps, you lived with roommates, reported to a boss, made new friends through work or hobbies, and met your future spouse.

A relationship is a bond, a mutual 'knowing' between two people. Such a bond can be familial, friendly, romantic, practical, or professional. Whoever the other person is, no matter who they are to you, they know some part of you.

As such, your best interests are open to them. This mutual 'knowing,' whether it is intensely close or simply by acquaintance, requires emotional intimacy, healthy boundaries, and, above all, trust. Without these things, the act of knowing someone and of letting ourselves be known can be incredibly vulnerable, in the worst of ways.

Unfortunately, many relationships don't naturally develop those skills and habits. Not because they are bad relationships, but because people don't have the knowledge or the tools to implement and practice them. Many people can't even imagine how their relationships could be different, or why they should change at all. They accept the discomfort, the emotional distance, and the lack of trust as normal and even expected—or they give up on the relationship altogether.

These things are not normal or innate aspects of any bond between two people. It is possible to connect to others in healthy and fulfilling ways. Nor is it always a sign that a relationship is wrong, broken, or doomed to failure if the people within it can't connect.

These things can be addressed, and the relationship can be repaired, even improved. It begins with a more fundamental understanding of the different types of relationships and their purposes in our lives. It also begins with a better understanding of what we, personally, want and expect from our relationships—how we approach them, how we hope to feel because of them, and where we wish they would flourish and bloom.

Different Types of Relationships

You may have experienced all of these kinds of relationships, or you may have formed only a few. Not all of them will hold positive memories for you, especially if your previous experiences with these bonds have been tainted by distrust or betrayal. But reading more about what, exactly, these connections are and how they should make us feel—even if you think you already know—can be incredibly helpful when learning how to build more successful connections with others.

Family

Family is, for many, the cornerstone of their lives. Our parents are our first introduction to the world. It is through them that we first encounter happiness or sadness, comforting hugs, music and words. They are— or should be—our first protection from all that is unpleasant or dangerous. They teach us how to take care of ourselves and our bodies, how to ride a bike, how to live!

Siblings, of course, present the incredible challenge of rivalry, companionship, annoyance, and protectiveness. They are our first friends and our bitterest enemies. For those without siblings, this sort of dynamic may manifest with childhood friends from the family who live down the street or other students at preschool. These sorts of connections can be tumultuous, but they often teach us more about the world and about ourselves than we realize even years later. For example, who better to teach you not to steal a toy than a sibling who will steal yours right back—or even worse, tell on you for stealing? You can bet that lesson stays ingrained up to adulthood.

Familial bonds often influence our perception of and expectations for other relationships in our lives; they are therefore the most important bonds to nurture with respect and love. The ideal familial relationships offer us unconditional stability and support, helping us to build our confidence, our self-worth, and our unique talents and interests, so that we can better succeed in the world.

Unfortunately, however, many do not have fulfilling or even worthwhile family bonds. If you are one of them, remember that you are no less deserving of this type of love than anyone else, and no less of a person for not having it.

Friends

The importance of familial attachments often, later in life, gives way to friendships. The family you choose, friendships are incredibly deep and unique connections that have the power to influence our interests, our habits, even our senses of fashion. The friends we make as children or as teenagers can make or break our self-esteem and even indicate our social statuses in school (where, for a while at least, social status is of the utmost importance to us).

As we get older, our friends become our lifelines, enhancing our experiences wherever we are—our dorm room at university, our place in a new city, our neighbors in the cul-de-sac. Good friends are sources of interesting conversation and laughter, keepers of heartbreaks and insecurities, and trustworthy allies.

Friendships can be even more everlasting than romantic attachments! As such, it's crucial to foster a strong, loving bond with your friends, one that can stand the test of time, distance, or age, as well as any emotional challenge.

Romantic relationships

Our first encounters with love are usually heady and intense. Whether you meet your first love in a homeroom or in the office, those feelings of attraction and adoration are intoxicating. Sometimes those feelings last; sometimes they don't. But we never stop searching and hoping for them, even after disappointment and heartbreak.

Given good luck and a fighting chance—and often after many false starts—infatuation blooms into mutual respect and love. Our romantic partners arguably know more about us than anyone else in the world. They can completely change the trajectories of our lives, from moving cross-country or starting a family. Such a bond is capable of bringing us to our highest highs and our lowest lows.

These sorts of connections, more than any other, require deep, abiding, and complete trust to thrive and last—hence why it is so important that we understand the best ways to foster emotional intimacy and trust, to set healthy boundaries, and to understand ourselves and our expectations.

Bosses and Co-workers

Finally, since most of us spend the majority of our days at work, we must focus on professional relationships.

These, too, deeply affect our lives. Co-workers, either those you chat with at the water cooler or work beside on your team, can determine your happiness and security at a workplace. Similarly, supervisors and managers should provide you with opportunities to refine and expand your skillset, as well as win raises and promotions.

These relationships can change a good day to a bad one, or vice versa, as well as foster your own professional success or failure. In an increasingly competitive world, where work is synonymous with passion and determinant of prosperity, this network must be cultivated and treated as respectfully as your bonds with family and friends. Even these relationships, though filled with less emotional closeness, can benefit from the tools and skills contained within this book.

Goals and Expectations

Now that we've defined the different sorts of relationships and their impacts on our lives, we must question our own expectations of and goals for these connections. It is not enough to simply say that we must have a good relationship—what does 'good' even mean?

To understand your own perception of a 'good' relationship, think critically about the following questions. Try to be as specific and honest with yourself as possible.

What about your relationships, currently, makes you feel happy and fulfilled? What are some points of dissatisfaction?

Take a close friend, for example. Perhaps they are incredibly fun to be around, but sometimes flaky when it comes to making plans. Or they share and love many of your interests, but can make jokes that hurt your feelings a little bit. Chances are, examples aside, you'll think of these pros and cons on your own.

Next: what is an 'ideal' relationship? With your mother, your best friend, your boss, your partner? What about that relationship is attractive to you? Where have you seen that ideal—in the media, in your friends' relationships?

Is the ideal you've thought of simply the opposite of a dissatisfying relationship in your life? Or is it a relationship you've always wanted but have never been able to find or achieve?

Most importantly, is your 'ideal' possible?

Many times, our expectations can get away from us. It's important to remember that if a relationship is unhappy, it's not lost forever. It is salvageable, even if it doesn't seem like it could ever be! It may be the case that the other person is failing you in some way, and if so, healthy and effective communication is a crucial skill to learn, one we will discuss in later chapters.

But it also may be that you are also at fault. There is nothing wrong with having high standards, but when those standards become impossible to meet, the entire relationship is in jeopardy.

For example, it's good to expect respect from your partner: communication about the status of your relationship, equally divided tasks, kindness and compassion. It can be destructive, however, to expect that your partner devotes all their time and energy to you, that they pay for every meal, or that they never once become irritated.

It is never wrong to expect respect from a human connection, because respect is a right to which we are all entitled. With respect comes trust, which is the subject of this book. What no one can demand, however, is codependency or sacrifice. This is an example of boundary-crossing, which we will discuss how to address later in the book. For now, simply ask yourself: Have I crossed anyone's boundaries without knowing? Do I expect too much?

Thoroughly and honestly examine your expectations of your relationships. Each type of relationship will have different answers to these questions, so make sure you take into account the different roles these connections play in your own life.

Take into account, too, the different goals of these connections. Professional relationships, of course, will have different goals than familial ones; from the former, you'd hope for a nice work environment and the opportunity to advance in your career, while from the latter, you'd hope for unconditional love and support. Your goal when making friends is to have companions in life, people with whom to eat brunch, watch films, and practice hobbies, people you can laugh and cry with. When dating, you look for all of that too, but also whether they are compatible with you long-term, whether you would want to tie your life to theirs, whether they would be a good parent to your prospective children.

Your specific goals for your specific relationships will affect both how you approach them now and how you approach them once you evaluate those relationships' effectiveness and value.

Ultimately, the questions of this chapter boil down to: What do you want from your relationships? What is stopping you from getting it?.

Chapter 2:

The Importance of Trust

A huge obstacle to the success of many relationships, of course, is trust—or the lack thereof. Without trust, how can respect and love truly flourish? If you cannot trust your romantic partner, for instance, you can never feel entirely at ease in their presence; doubt will taint every perception of them and their actions, as well as every interaction you have with them. If this goes on for too long, the relationship will become defined by suspicion and betrayal—not by respect or love, as any connection should be.

Anyone who has questioned their friend's intentions, disbelieved about their partner's promises, or felt uneasy about their superior's goals knows how horrible those feelings are. Suspicion is a snake, slithering its way into your mind and your heart. It hisses to you of insecurity, anger, and fear, louder and louder, until you cannot help but believe it. The snake wraps itself around you and squeezes until you can no longer breathe. By then, whether the suspicion is deserved or not, the relationship is suffering; you simply can't mistrust someone and simultaneously give of yourself to them in the way any good relationship demands.

Oppressive and nearly impossible to escape, suspicion has a way of tainting every other relationship in our lives, ones we'd never questioned before doubting this particular one. By then, true human connection feels pointless, dangerous even, because it becomes painfully clear that by caring for another, you open your heart to them; and they have every opportunity to hurt you, should they so choose.

By that point, not only do you sabotage your own relationships with your suspicions: you sabotage yourself, closing yourself off from the joy and fulfillment of respecting and loving others, and being respected and loved in return. By expecting the worst, you cannot see, cannot appreciate and cannot believe the good.

But truly successful and healthy relationships really don't have room for suspicion. They are built on mutual commitment to respect and care, so much that the way they function is geared towards building and maintaining trust. It becomes so much a part of how we treat each other that it's impossible to separate the emotional attachment from the bond itself, the way we treat each other; they become intertwined.

So what is trust, really? How can we quantify and define it? And more importantly, how do we go about establishing it?

What is Trust?

Merriam-Webster's dictionary defines trust as "assured reliance on the character, ability, strength, or truth of someone" or "one in which confidence is placed" (Merriam-Webster, n.d., c). The second definition is perhaps the most telling.

Trust is confidence. In another person. In yourself. And confidence shapes everything.

Take the definition of confidence: "the quality or state of being certain" (Merriam-Webster, n.d., b).

Confidence is, from the very beginning of our lives, a trait we strive toward in ourselves. Having the confidence, for example, to give our first presentation in the fifth grade. Having the confidence to ask out a pretty girl. Pursuing a master's degree, applying for a job, parenting.

Of course, for many of these things, you don't need confidence; just determination or bravery. But inherent in all of these things is the hope of success, and with that hope does come confidence—for in some small way, simply by pursuing a date or giving a presentation, you believe you will succeed.

You believe that you are intelligent enough to present a compelling presentation and receive a good grade; that you are charming enough to attract someone's interest; that you are capable enough to perform well in a job, or be a good parent.

Without that belief in yourself, you may put forth minimal effort in these pursuits, or even avoid them altogether, in order to avoid what you *believe* will happen: failure.

Confidence in ourselves, or lack thereof, is rooted in belief. So, is trust in another person. When you trust someone, your confidence in them is high; you believe in them. You believe in who they have shown themselves to be. You believe in their intentions towards you.

In this way, trust is the highest compliment you can give someone.

So, when you doubt someone, or find you cannot trust them at all, you fear their failure. You fear your own failure to see who they really are. You fear pain.

That is why, in many ways, betrayal hurts so deeply. Your greatest fears have come true. Your belief in that person has been shattered; everything you know about them, and even about yourself, seems to be wrong. They have failed you, and you have failed yourself for believing wrongly, for giving your trust to— seemingly—the wrong person.

Conversely, if you have been the betrayer, causing this broken confidence, this shattered belief, in the other person is the source of your guilt and shame. You have failed two people: the person who trusted you, and yourself, for causing such pain and being the source of that failure.

Different Kinds of Trust

Of course, there are different kinds of betrayal, and thus different kinds of trust. These variations come from the diverse types of relationships we form throughout our lives.

A professional relationship, for instance, carries specific expectations with regard to loyalty, respect, and responsibility. An entry-level employee, perhaps, expects their superior to help them to learn the ropes, to give them opportunities to grow, and to speak well of them if they have performed admirably. Their superior, in return, expects the employee to complete their tasks on time, to cooperate and collaborate with other members of the team, and to remain with the company long enough to make their training worthwhile.

This kind of trust, more than any other perhaps, is grounded in mutual benefit. The employee, by remaining true to their employer's trust, receives a paycheck for their work and presumably has the chance to rise in status later on. The employer's department runs more smoothly and efficiently because of the employee's work, and productivity rises.

Such mutual confidence is, for the most part, built and fulfilled for practical gain. It is not an emotional kind of trust, but a material one—whereas in a romantic relationship, trust is absolutely grounded in emotion.

All kinds of emotion, in fact. Romantic bonds are among the most complex we can form. Trust in a romantic partner is based on your affection for their personality, your emotional vulnerability with them, and your long-term commitment to each other, as well as any practical concerns you share, such as homeownership or joint bank accounts. Not to mention children!

You trust a partner not only to treat you well, comfort your sadness, keep your confidence, and remain loyal, but also to share equally of your joint assets and help make ends meet.

Any kind of betrayal in a romantic relationship—dishonesty, infidelity—will affect both your emotional and your practical trust. After all, the point of a romantic connection is not for practical gain as in a professional boss-employee relationship, but to attain happiness and belonging.

When distrust and disloyalty jeopardize that sense of happiness and belonging in a romantic bond, the loss of trust—of confidence—is devastating. It can feel particularly impossible to rebuild, especially in the case of infidelity.

Any trust, in fact, once broken, can seem broken forever. But understanding exactly what sort of trust characterizes your relationships is the key to building a strong foundation, which hopefully will not crumble when faced with treachery, and will provide a framework to preventing such disappointments in the first place.

So think clearly about how you trust those in your life; what, exactly, you trust in and about the people you love. What parts of you are vulnerable to them, and under their protection, as it were?

Benefits of Growing Trust

Needless to say, you do not trust someone immediately after meeting them. You usually don't even fully trust them after meeting them five times, or ten.

Trust must be earned; this takes consistent time and effort, not only when the relationship is just beginning but also years down the line. You must be trustworthy, over and over, as well as choose to trust another, over and over, as they prove themselves trustworthy in return. *Maintaining* trust is just as important as earning it in the first place.

Nevertheless, you should never enter a relationship and consider trust to be an optional part of it. Hopefully these chapters so far have explained that trust is an essential part of a relationship; it is as basic and fundamental as respect or love.

If you feel as if you cannot trust someone in particular, and cannot imagine ever trusting that person, your relationship with them is unfortunately not worth your time. It will only sow anxiety, doubt, and fear in your mind and heart. A complete lack of trust in one person will most assuredly inspire distrust in others as well, even those who don't deserve it.

While you may not always be able to extricate yourself from a connection with someone who is untrustworthy, it is best to always remember why you cannot trust them, and to take measures to protect yourself both against further deception and betrayal as well as possible gaslighting.

Above all, you deserve to have fulfilling, secure relationships in your life. You deserve the joy of surrounding yourself with good, reliable people. Not to feel anxious or doubtful of their affection and intentions, but to have confidence that they want only the best for you and that they trust you as well.

There is no end to the benefits of giving your loved ones a chance, and no end to the thrill of proving your own trustworthiness to them in return.

Because relationships founded on trust, of course, make you happier. They make each day more fulfilling, whether it is a good or a bad one; they provoke tears of laughter and wipe tears of sadness. Such bonds are the difference between loneliness and belonging, and often between fear and bravery.

Having dependable friends and family makes it easier to face difficult challenges, knowing you have a support system; trusting your co-workers to do their part in a big project makes the process and the work much less stressful.

Proving yourself to be trustworthy, too, has benefits. Not only will it make your relationships richer and deeper, strengthening your emotional intimacy and closeness, it will enhance your confidence in *yourself*. Because often, what others believe of us, we believe, too.

So when our best friends come to us with their greatest fears or deepest secrets, we too come to believe we are good listeners and reliable secret keepers. Or when our boss approaches us with a sensitive project, the most important one we've yet been assigned, we too can believe we are capable, intelligent, and skilled.

Knowing that others think us worthy of trust, as well as respect and love, is a tremendous boost to self-esteem. We can be proud of ourselves then; we can look at who we are and what we do with satisfaction and pleasure.

In short, with trust as an integral, non-negotiable part of our relationships, life is simply better. But what do you do when trust feels impossible? When it disappears altogether?

Chapter 3:
Attachment Theory

To better understand the answers to these questions, or to better understand our relationships in the first place, a useful place to begin is John Bowlby's theory of attachment.

Beginning in the 1950s, Bowlby studied child development and began to apply his findings to adult relationships, developing his "attachment theory." Essentially, it is the idea that the function of our relationships with our parents when we are very young can determine and affect how we approach other relationships, later in life. Caregivers' behavior "contributes to and forms the way a child [and later an adult] perceives close relationships" (The Attachment Project, para. 7).

What this means is that when a child's needs—either emotional or physical—are unmet, or met wrongly, by their caregivers, the impression of that experience lingers. We remember our hurts. And, ultimately, we apply the experience of *being* hurt—how it felt, in what circumstances it occurred—to all our other relationships.

For example, do you often find yourself frustrated by your own reaction to problems or arguments? Do you wonder why your romantic relationships keep ending the same way?

Do you have problems with clinginess or jealousy? Are you plagued by the suspicion that you are the most involved and committed in a relationship, or do you find yourself backing off from any potential relationship, even though you want it dearly?

If the answer to any of these questions is yes, that does not mean your caregivers are terrible people and that you are broken. Most of our caregivers have wanted the best for us and tried their hardest to provide it.

But the unfortunate fact is: it is extremely difficult to raise a child. No matter how good a person you are, no matter how well-intentioned, you will fail your child in some way. Ultimately, very few parents are their child's idea of a perfect parent, simply because all parents, and all children, are unique individuals with unique needs.

Rather, approach the analysis of these 4 attachment styles as a way to more deeply understand yourself and your approach to relationships—in order to foster healthier and more meaningful bonds. Not to unnecessarily project, not to place blame, but to be better children, better siblings, better coworkers, better friends, better partners. Better people, who constantly seek to self-improve.

Attachment theory above all is a way to understand ourselves and to understand why we constantly find ourselves making the same mistakes, repeating the same patterns, or attracting the same kinds of people—even when we don't want to.

The Four Styles of Attachment

So what are the four styles of attachment? Bowlby defines them as anxious (preoccupied), avoidant (dismissive), disorganized (fearful-avoidant), and secure. Confused already? Don't worry; below, we'll go through them one by one.

Keep in mind, as you read the descriptions, that you may not perfectly fit one style, and that in fact you may switch from one style or another with different people. Again, these styles are meant only as a tool to better understand your own subconscious perspectives and approaches, not to fit anyone into a single box.

Rather, our exploration of these attachment styles is to help you recognize your own behavioral patterns, habits that may be weakening or hurting your relationships, and thus to have the power to change those patterns and habits.

Anxious (Preoccupied)

The anxious, or preoccupied, attachment style is defined by—you guessed it—anxiety. Anxiety about being alone or abandoned, about not being enough for your partner, and about your partner's investment in the relationship.

Those with an anxious attachment style typically have low self-esteem, but hold those they love and respect in high regard. As such, they believe that the attention and love of their partner (or friend, or sibling, or boss) is a "remedy" to their anxiety. The more frequent and obvious the outward signs of dedication and devotion, the less intense the feelings of rejection, fear, and insufficiency.

This is, above all, a pattern of behavior that is rooted in insecurity. It is a manifestation of the belief that romantic love—or the friendship of someone you admire, or the approval of a boss—will make you whole. That it will make you belong. That it will give you meaning, and suddenly fix everything that is wrong in your life and in yourself.

No relationship, and indeed no single person, can do that for someone else. It is impossible.

And so it should be! Our sense of self should never be dependent upon the goodwill and affection of another person. When it is, any absence, or perceived disinterest, from anyone we love can cause a knee-jerk, desperate reaction. We may become clingy or demanding, causing the other to feel suffocated or insufficient themselves. We may neglect our other relationships, our responsibilities, and our personal hobbies in order to favor one single bond.

When someone with an anxious attachment style cannot find a relationship to fill the void they perceive in themselves, they may even feel unmoored, lost, and worthless—as if their identity does not matter, or that they have no identity at all, without another to acknowledge and affirm it.

This kind of attachment style, which places our self-worth into the hands of another, can so easily lead to disappointment and pain—if not codependency, manipulation, or abuse. Expecting another to affirm our own importance, at the very least, places them in a very uncomfortable, unrealistic, and ultimately, unattainable position.

No one can completely fulfill another person. Expecting that they do so will only lead to more disappointment, and more cycles of insufficiency and desperation. Additionally, when we give others the power to define our own worth and importance, we give them ultimate power over us, to honor—or indeed hurt—us as they please.

An anxious attachment style, though involving placing trust in others, is the exact opposite of trust, because this attachment style lacks any trust in *oneself*.

Avoidant (Dismissive)

On the other end of the spectrum is the avoidant, or dismissive, attachment style. People with this attachment style may refuse to place trust in anyone whatsoever, because they do not believe they have to, or even that anyone else deserves their trust.

They think of themselves as "lone wolves": strong, independent, and self-sufficient (The Attachment Project, para. 14). Above all, they avoid depending on others and feel uncomfortable and claustrophobic when others depend on them. While those with an anxious attachment style have low self-esteem but high belief in others, those who approach relationships with an avoidant attachment style have high self-esteem, but a very low regard for others.

This manifests in an expectation of disappointment or hurt, coupled with a habitual avoidance of any emotional intimacy or vulnerability. People with this sort of style may even suppress their own emotions when confronting a situation with high tensions or feelings.

Just as the anxious attachment style depends too much on others, the avoidant attachment style depends too much on the self. Those who find themselves approaching relationships with this style may, consciously or not, undervalue the importance of trust and relationships in their lives.

So, just as the anxious attachment style sabotages itself by placing too much importance on the opinion of others, so too does the avoidant attachment style sabotage itself by purposefully distancing and isolating from others altogether.

This attachment style, too, lacks a vital sense of trust: this time in others.

Disorganized (Fearful-Avoidant)

The disorganized, or fearful-avoidant, attachment style is a combination of the anxious and avoidant—if you couldn't tell by the name.

The concept of a relationship, any kind of a relationship, is to the disorganized attachment style both ideal and terrifying. People with this style *do* want to connect to others—they just can't seem to find the courage or strength to try. They fear getting hurt, so they avoid attachment altogether.

So this attachment style combines the insecurity of the anxious style and the isolation of the avoidant style. The end result is the same: self-sabotage.

Secure

Lastly, but certainly not least, we come to the *secure* attachment style. People who approach their relationships with this style are the antithesis of all the others. They do not fear expressing their emotions; rather, they do so gladly and openly. They welcome others' confidence in them, and readily trust others. They approach disagreements with honesty and humility. And though they may thrive in relationships, they don't fear being alone.

People with this attachment style, above all, have secure self-esteem, which neither depends on nor mistrusts others.

You have to wonder if this kind of person could even exist, right?

It can seem impossible. Everyone has insecurities; everyone is afraid of vulnerability in some way and wary of trusting others. Everyone dreads being alone.

These things are only natural. They only become problematic when they become *patterns*. When they regularly, significantly impact your important relationships.

Don't be discouraged if you recognize those patterns in yourself. The good news is, these attachment styles are not set in stone—you *can* change your attachment style, at any time, at any age, and in any relationship.

Attachment Styles and Job Performance

Although it is natural and easy to apply Bowlby's theory of attachment to romantic relationships, it may be more productive to instead apply them to our habits and behaviors at work.

In this section we'll explore how to apply the theory to our own work styles, and how to change them in order to become more productive, effective, and successful— not only at work, but also at home.

For example, those with the anxious attachment style may have an acute fear of disappointing or upsetting others. This can manifest in a compulsion to check email incessantly, seeking out problems and hoping to appease them quickly (Saunders, 2018, para. 5). They may also, when faced with negative or merely *neutral* feedback on their performance, fear the worst: that they have utterly failed at their task, even that they are soon to be replaced or fired.

Clearly, this type of approach to work is unhealthy at best and unproductive at worst. Such anxiety surrounding the workplace, and our own work performance, can only serve to undermine both. When we have no trust in our ability, nor in our contribution to our workplace, the power of both decreases.

For this attachment style, then, the best solution is to consciously, consistently set boundaries, both for others and for ourselves, and to monitor our self-talk. If you have trouble saying no to demands to work late, even when you already have plans for the night, commit yourself to setting that boundary: you will leave at a reasonable time.

If you catch yourself constantly devaluing your own capability, thinking things like "They probably hated my work," or "I'm not useful to this team at all," try to reroute your thoughts. Remind yourself that you have tried your hardest on your work; if you make a mistake, acknowledge that you are human but also that you have excelled in another area. Above all, realize that negative thoughts are not *facts*. They are merely perceptions. As such, we can change them, morphing a negative situation into a neutral or even a positive one, and strengthening our own confidence in return.

We will discuss boundaries and self-talk in more depth in Chapters 8 and 11 respectively, but for now, simply remember that it is absolutely in your power to take more control of your life and of your happiness.

Conversely, an employee with an avoidant attachment style may overvalue their own work and ability and undervalue those of their colleagues or even their superiors. They may even miss deadlines, or do the work in a different way than prescribed because they feel their idea is better (Saunders, 2018, para. 12).

Such an employee must do the opposite work than the one with an anxious attachment style; they must recognize others' worth, effort, and ability, as well as the importance of other ideas in the workplace. There is an emphasis on teams for a reason: more diverse minds mean more diverse ideas and approaches, and, ultimately, better results.

Again, someone who approaches their work with a disorganized attachment style is a mix of the previous two. They have the "fear of those with anxious attachment without the confidence that they can make things right" (Saunders, 2018, para. 16). Unlike an employee with an anxious attachment style, these employees would not rush to solve a problem in order to appease anyone's disapproval or anger; rather, they would try to avoid the problem altogether, never face it, pretend it does not exist.

These employees may feel easily overwhelmed and have little confidence in their ability to overcome obstacles. They may also tend to procrastinate projects, questioning why they should even try.

For employees with this attachment style, following self-care methods is crucial. To overcome disruptive anxiety, it is best to find ways to distract your brain from it entirely—focusing on the five senses, completing a small puzzle, going for a quick walk.

Furthermore, breaking tasks into small, manageable pieces can help to lessen feelings of stress. An important project due a week from now, which you haven't even begun, can become five, ten, fifteen small tasks, spread throughout the day and easily ticked off a list.

What all of these attachment styles lack, again, is secure self-esteem. A secure employee, in this case, approaches their work with calmness and belief in their own competence. They do the best they can on their tasks as they arrive; they do not hesitate to set boundaries around their own time; and above all, they do not fear feedback.

Rather, employees with a secure attachment seek to maintain that equilibrium, and so they *ask* for feedback. They consistently check in with their colleagues, superiors, and clients, and adjust their own work performance and habits accordingly.

Again, you may recognize yourself in one of these attachment styles—or you may be all four at once, depending on the setting. Think about how each specific attachment style can manifest itself in different relationships or situations. For example, someone with an avoidant attachment style may avoid making new friends, or disdain the ones they already have.

Indeed, you may identify more as a securely attached employee, but feel you are avoidant in your romantic relationships. You may approach new friends with an anxious attachment style while you approach family with a disorganized one.

Whatever the case, it's important to remember that attachment styles can above all change. Anyone can become secure in any kind of relationship, given the chance and the tools.

So, how do we change our attachment style?

Cultivating a Secure Attachment Style

The key here is healthy communication. You'll find it is a recurring theme throughout the book, and it is certainly a theme in both descriptions of the secure attachment style explained earlier in this chapter. Those with a secure attachment style approach communication as a necessary, good thing, with openness and commitment to listening.

We must first communicate with ourselves—honestly, without judgment—about how we have approached and affected our relationships in the past. No one wants to admit that they have perhaps introduced unhealthy patterns into their friendships or romantic partnerships, even worse cultivated them.

But remember how unrealistic the secure attachment style seems? Consistent communication, high self-esteem, willingness to trust and be vulnerable—these things are not easy. They can seem downright impossible.

The process of becoming a well-adjusted person takes time and effort, and not a small amount of help. So remember that you have just begun that journey. You cannot blame yourself for not having the tools before, when you have only now encountered them.

So: look at yourself, your past relationships, your thought and emotion patterns surrounding those relationships, and how well those relationships have flourished—or not. (And remember, don't blame your parents too much for these things; as adults, it's our responsibility to grow.)

What is affecting how you relate to others? How do you allow others to relate to you?

And once you have taken the steps to improve those relations, how can you keep yourself from falling back into the same old patterns? Unfortunately, just as people can change their attachment styles for the better, so too can they find those styles have changed for the worse.

If that happens, or if indeed you find yourself in an already unhealthy pattern, the next step is acknowledging, and believing, what you think and feel.

Chapter 4:
Signs of Discontent

Have you ever had a heavy pit in your stomach on your way to meet someone, but never figured out why? Have you noticed someone pulling away from you, but been unsure if you were just overthinking it?

This chapter is all about those little signs, and how to read them.

If life were perfect, relationships would be easy. Connecting to others would be a simple matter of getting to know them and appreciating who they are, and we would never cause each other discomfort or pain, least of all on purpose. We would always be happy, and no relationship would ever grow stagnant or prickly. And most of all, we would never lose anyone; no relationship that is important to us would ever fail.

Unfortunately, life is not perfect. All too often, we wake up one day and realize that our relationship is over before we even knew it was in trouble. All too often, the problem is in *ourselves*, and we never even recognized it before it changed everything in our lives forever.

And after the fact, we can drive ourselves crazy trying to pinpoint where it all went wrong, cursing our blindness or our stupidity. We can blame ourselves for losing someone so special to us.

Missing signs of dissatisfaction in a relationship has nothing to do with blindness or stupidity. It's not a moral failing, just a lack of awareness and the tools with which we recognize and believe these signs. Here in this chapter, we'll give you both.

There's a veritable grocery list of ways in which unhappiness in our relationships can manifest, both physically and emotionally, and in ourselves and the other person. It's so easy to write them off as tiredness, unrelated stress, illness, or anything else. And sometimes, of course, that's all it is. Everyone has their ups and their downs, and when one person's unique life circumstances affect a relationship, it really is nothing personal.

But of course, the trick is to know when these signs really are nothing, and when, in fact, they are symptoms of discontent between you.

We must learn to believe what our emotions and bodies tell us when it comes to our relationships. To tell the difference between overthinking and intuition. Because sometimes, whether we know it or not, our relationships just aren't working. But usually, the signs are there, if we can only see and accept them.

These signs may be small (emotions or sensations) or they may be big, like strange absences or more frequent arguments. They may be easy to spot or incredibly difficult to recognize. And, crucially, they might be very easy to address and solve.

Or they might not.

Recognizing signs of discontent in a suffering relationship is, unfortunately, only the first step of saving it. The work only begins here—and make no mistake, it is work. The next chapters will discuss how to address discontent and even betrayal, by introducing ways to forgive and reconnect, how to set boundaries, how to be emotionally vulnerable, and how to communicate productively and respectfully.

But before all that, let's just explore how to tell if anything is going wrong in the first place.

What Does Discontent Look Like?

Discontent can be both physical and emotional, and it can also be internal or external. This does, admittedly, make it confusing. Especially when any of these signs can be attributed to so many other things! Even if you recognize *half* of these signs and behaviors in yourself or someone else, they could be completely unrelated to your relationship with each other.

This guide is not meant to make you overthink your relationships or to suddenly doubt everyone you know, even yourself. Chances are, if you're reading this book, you already know that something is wrong, even if you can't exactly pinpoint it. In this chapter we only want to help you pinpoint that wrongness.

Physical Signs

Physically, dissatisfaction and discomfort can show themselves in a number of ways. Anxiety is the biggest and most noticeable of these.

Anxiety feels different for everyone, and one person can even feel different manifestations of anxiety in different circumstances or because of various reasons.

Sweating, trouble sleeping, dizziness, tightness in the chest or shortness of breath, headaches, and more are common signs of anxiety (Smith et al., 2019, para. 5). Additionally, tension in our muscles, our jaws, or our hands can all be signs of stress or nervousness.

Now, again, these sorts of sensations may have nothing to do with your relationship. But, if you regularly feel physical anxiety, it can be helpful to think about the circumstances in which you do.

Have you been feeling butterflies in your stomach whenever you see someone lately, someone who never caused such feelings before? Have you been unable to physically relax in the presence of an old friend or a committed partner? If so, there may be some sort of correlation that is worth exploring.

Additionally, more noticeable physical distress can also indicate emotional pain, such as crying. Have you been crying more often lately, for no apparent reason? Or especially when you are with someone, or have just left their company?

Physical symptoms of stress have many causes, and for that reason we often write them off, especially if we already suffer from conditions such as anxiety. But it's good to remember that our bodies do speak to us. All of these signs can indicate more serious emotional problems in a relationship, be it familial or professional, so it can be useful to examine these sensations for a deeper cause if we think there is one.

Especially if other signs appear at the same time.

Emotional Signs

Now, emotional signs are often easier to recognize than physical ones, but they are much harder to believe—precisely because they are emotional. They are mostly just thoughts, after all, or arguments, which all people in relationships have sometimes. Most of us don't want to see ghosts where there are none, and so we talk ourselves out of worry and convince ourselves that, no, we're just overreacting.

Take this sign of discontent, in a romantic relationship: daydreaming about being single. Who hasn't done this, especially after our partner has done something to really annoy or enrage us? But constant daydreaming, and especially constant reminiscing about *old* relationships, can be a sign of major dissatisfaction with our partners (Mateo, 2019, para. 30). In a healthy relationship, one that truly makes us happy, being *single* would not appear to be a better prospect or alternative.

Similarly, when we purposefully prioritize other relationships over another, it can mean that at heart, we don't want to spend time with that person. If we find ourselves reluctant to be in someone's company, or avoiding it altogether, it's a sign that, perhaps, we no longer *enjoy* being in that relationship. If we enjoyed it, we'd seek it out! So this is a serious indication that something may be going wrong between you.

These are more subtle emotional signals of relationship problems; now onto the more obvious ones. We often notice these signs, but we justify or even accept them rather than interpreting them as the symptoms of discontent that they really are.

For instance, the temptation to secretly read a romantic partner's private messages, and especially the inability to stop once you've started. As we'll discuss later in the book, privacy is an important and inherent right, one that all of us are entitled to. Ignoring that boundary, whether it's justified or not, is a form of disrespect. And even if you do ask for permission to read someone's messages, the desire to do so nearly always indicates that your trust in them is severely lacking.

Beyond suspicion or distrust, we may feel anger or even contempt that we can't seem to shake. It may feel harder to look past small mistakes such as a friend's lateness to an event, or a partner not pulling their own weight with the household chores. We may start to feel anger for past misdeeds or arguments, or develop new grudges that we just can't shake.

When it's difficult for us to forgive the people in our lives, especially for petty and relatively unimportant things, it's not just that the other person is annoying, or that we have a temper. It's usually a warning that we aren't as happy in the relationship as we once were.

All of these emotions point to a sense of having been wronged, and they may be even more intense if our family, friends, partners, or coworkers show us little gratitude or appreciation. We want the people in our lives to really care for us, so the feeling of being taken for granted can be a horrible blow to our self-esteem and stir up resentment, which in turn can destabilize the relationship itself.

Even worse is an increase in criticisms or judgments. Repeated negative commentary is a huge indication that a relationship is struggling. No matter the type, a relationship should always be founded on and treated with respect: being mindful of each other's feelings, providing constructive feedback if someone does something wrong, and always remembering that they are worthy fellow human beings. Nitpicking, sarcasm, and cruelty should never define how we treat each other.

Of course, fights will happen sometimes; tensions rise and tempers flare. It's only natural, especially in a close bond like a romantic relationship. But picking fights with a partner all the time, or vice versa, is not normal.

Like many of the other behaviors on this list, it's a signal that something is going wrong between you. Frustration easily boils over, yes, but romantic relationships are defined above all by love; hoping to argue with your partner, to make them angry, or even to hurt them, are *not* acts of love, but just the opposite.

Paradoxically, *not* fighting can be a sign of discontentment, too. It is, after all, only natural that we argue in a relationship. The amount of time spent together, the clash of different opinions and wants, the balance of responsibility and duty, all of these can cause friction and disagreement between romantic partners. In a good relationship, however, arguing can solve these problems and bring you closer together.

But when it just seems easier not to say anything, or worse, when you don't care enough to argue at all— either your ability to communicate with each other is suffering greatly, or the relationship has gone stagnant. You can't reach each other, or the problems between you have made it so that you don't even want to.

These problems may be things you've noticed yourself doing, patterns you've noticed in someone else's behavior, or a mixture of both. Again, one or even many of these things are not always indications that your relationship is horrible or that it's doomed to fail. And any problems may be much more complex and unique than any of these examples.

Again, this is only a guide to help you see possible weak spots in a relationship, so that eventually, you can strengthen it. The bottom line is this: Do you feel lonely in any of your relationships? Do you feel like your connection with someone else is less of a bond and more of a burden? Do you feel like you have no voice, no true understanding or companionship?

If so, you should trust these feelings. They are telling you something.

Accepting Your Perceptions

So, if any of the above examples struck a chord with you, it's time to accept those feelings. You are not stupid, and neither are you too sensitive. You are not overthinking. You must believe in your own perceptions.

But how?

What helps best, in such cases, is talking to others. Not to the person in the relationship in question, not just yet. But to other, more impartial listeners.

If the problem is with a family member, a friend or a partner is a great candidate to ask for advice. If it is a friend or a partner, then ask a family member! And so on. Though, hopefully, everyone in our lives will feel a certain protectiveness over our feelings and our happiness, ask the other person to be as objective as possible when listening to your concerns. Ask them to consider the issues as fairly as they can.

Just like we can never *directly* see our faces—we can only see ourselves through a mirror or a photo, neither of them as true to life as plain eye vision—we can never accurately see our own thoughts, emotions, and lives. Our emotions cause and affect our thought processes in ways we can't always recognize; our thoughts change the way we perceive people and events. In effect, we blind ourselves. So, we should always welcome any external, objective input.

In this way, therapy is a fantastic tool. As we explain in other chapters, there is no shame in attending or needing therapy; just like dentists are best qualified to tend to our teeth, therapists are trained professionals who can guide us through our own emotions and thoughts, often better than we ourselves can. And they are the ultimate impartial listeners.

If, after speaking with a trusted friend or a therapist, you find that your worries and intuitions still seem right to you, then it's time to approach the other person. Later on, we'll discuss in more detail how to do so. For the time being, though, just remember: don't overreact, don't accuse, just believe in your own feelings. You're completely allowed to feel them.

Chapter 5:

Overcoming Betrayal

Life is not perfect, and neither are people. No one alive is without fault. Making mistakes, small or big, and even making a lot of them, does not mean we are evil; it means we are human.

However, it is easy to expect that those you love will never make mistakes. We often put those we love on a pedestal. We find them utterly incredible, and so it follows that *they must be* utterly incredible, always in and in every way.

But as we all must know, this is an impossible expectation.

Still, no matter how well we know that objectively, no one is perfect, we almost cannot help ourselves in expecting someone to be. The disappointment that follows when we discover that a loved one is not so incredible, but can even be awful, is bitter and deep. Such disappointment can sour and ruin a relationship before you've even truly processed it.

And it is so easy to condemn someone when they have made a mistake, no matter how much we love them. Because they *were* incredible! We thought they were, least. So, we were wrong all along, more fools we; the person we love is awful and we do not want to love them anymore; and the relationship is better left behind us.

See how easily those thoughts turn to one another? A relationship is so easily destroyed by distrust and disloyalty, even in cases where it can be saved. And so, too, those thoughts will turn to other relationships: You may wonder, naturally, if someone else will disappoint you in the same way, if they too will hurt you. And so all your relationships become unsteady and unstable, cracking the foundation on which you stand.

We must do our best to break that line of thinking before it even starts, to pull it out from the root. No one is perfect, and it is unfair to believe or expect that they are—especially when we, ourselves, want the benefit of the doubt. We, too, want forgiveness for our mistakes. Because of course we all make them.

So how do we forgive, when it feels impossible? How do we trust again at all?

If someone is truly important to you, and your connection to them truly meaningful, it cannot and will not secure your own happiness to leave them or abandon all hope in the relationship. As we said before, we must not be afraid of hard work.

Sometimes it really is impossible, and your bond has been truly broken by betrayal. You have made yourself vulnerable to the wrong person. Unfortunately, this happens. So, in the last part of this chapter we'll explore how to say goodbye to a relationship in a fulfilling way, with no regrets and as little pain as possible.

Mostly, though, we will emphasize the importance of compassion in either of these cases, both for yourself and for the other person. Because we know that we, too, are prone to making the same mistakes that we condemn others for making. We know we have faults. (At least, we should.) It is best to remember that as we analyze how to face and process our emotions when faced with betrayal, how to contextualize betrayal in our lives, and how to decide what to do about it.

Acknowledging Your Sense of Betrayal

When a betrayal happens, of course, one of the hardest things about it is believing that it has happened at all. Everything we knew and believed is suddenly upended, because someone we love *chose* to hurt us. It's that choice which is so hard to understand. How could they have done this? *Why* would they have done this?

These questions are incessant and impossible to ignore. And from them, come even more questions: Did we ever really know this person at all? Did they ever really love or respect us, even though we loved and respected them so much?

These questions are almost too horrible to contemplate. And undoubtedly, the way you answer them will be affected by your emotions.

Having experienced a betrayal, it goes without saying that you are in pain. Whether it is a friend, a partner, or a co-worker who has betrayed us, the feelings of disbelief, heartache, and anger that come hand-in-hand with betrayal are horrible and earth-shattering. And from those emotions spawn others, more insidious, which serve to erode our trust in the person who betrayed us even more.

Let's walk through them one at a time.

"I don't deserve this! I was always so kind and giving towards them."

This statement is a classic example of self-righteousness, or inflating our own sense of self at the expense of others. When faced with betrayal, it is a defense mechanism to reject our feelings of belittlement and unimportance by instead insisting upon our own goodness—to the point that it becomes unrealistic.

No one wants to believe they have been betrayed or that they are at all deserving of betrayal. And so, when it happens, we automatically comfort ourselves by insisting that no, we didn't deserve it, because *we* are incredible! So how dare they do this to *us*?

We become saints, perfect people who have never done wrong in our lives and who have been horribly and cruelly mistreated. And our betrayers have undoubtedly mistreated us!

But this kind of emotion, and these kinds of statements, skew our understanding of the situation. They make our betrayers into evil caricatures of themselves.

When trying to accept betrayal—not to forgive it, not to move past it, but simply to accept that a betrayal has happened—it is crucial that we keep it in perspective.

We must try to remember who exactly we are, even though our ideas about the other person have been altered.

"They're the scum of the earth. I hate them."

Resentment: the last thing we need when trying to objectively understand betrayal and decide how to confront it. Resentment is the opposite side of the coin to self-righteousness; indeed, they often go hand-in-hand.

When we self-aggrandize in order to mitigate our own pain, we lessen the other person's value in return. By instantly turning against them, and using their misdeeds to define them, we invalidate everything about them that we love. We also make ourselves dishonest, by burying our more productive emotions and covering them with blind hate. It becomes difficult then to see the relationship and the situation objectively.

Of course, it's natural to be angry and resentful, even hard not to be. Your feelings are always valid, and many times, anger can be cathartic and full of clarity. And, yes, you may have been hurt by someone who really isn't worth your time after all. Even then, when anger clouds your judgment of a situation, it is unhelpful.

"I knew they would betray me. Everyone always does in the end."

Finally, self-pity. Everyone does it, especially when faced with disappointment and hurt. From hearing cruel remarks from a high school clique to getting passed over for a promotion, self-pity is our often instant response to hardship, as well as the response hardest to shake.

Unlike self-righteousness or resentment, self-pity is not a defense mechanism; rather, it is a way to hurt *ourselves*, to dig the barbs in a little deeper, and wallow in our negative emotions. By indulging in self-pity, we intensify our own pain.

Needless to say, savoring our own pain in such a way is not conducive to coping with problems or accepting them as they are. Like the other responses, self-pity clouds our perception of a situation. Rather than see a problem for what it is, we see a heartless, irredeemable enemy, and we interpret ourselves as a weak, powerless underdog, doomed to failure and fated for pain.

If we come to truly believe our self-pity, to truly believe that we are perpetual victims, we risk manifesting that belief into reality: we *expect* others to hurt us, so much so that we don't even try to build meaningful relationships or attempt to fix those we already have when they go wrong.

When we believe in our own self-pity, we self-sabotage. We convince ourselves we are victims and that others are right for treating us as such: that we don't even deserve happiness.

We must believe more of ourselves than constant martyrdom. Even if a betrayal cuts deep, it does not make us powerless. And no one ever deserves to be treated with disrespect or cruelty.

Above all, we all have a right to happiness, as well as the chance to build it. So, don't steal it from yourself! Rather than fall into the trap of self-righteousness, resentment, and above all self-pity, practice *acceptance*.

Easier said than done, of course. True acceptance requires that you go through those pesky five stages of grief, from denial to anger to depression, when in fact the five stages are never so linear; we jump from one to the other, forward and back. It is all part of the healing process, which cannot be rushed.

But acceptance can be fought for, in our minds if not our hearts. One of the best ways to do this is to practice objectivity. And objectivity often comes as impartiality. Rather than replay the betrayal over and over in your head or wallow endlessly in your pain, write out what happened as if it had happened to someone else.

Say you lent a friend some clothing, and she returned it covered in rips and stains, absolutely ruined. It would be difficult to approach her and think of anything but your anger and hurt at her disrespect and carelessness. And so a surmountable problem becomes insurmountable.

Instead, write it down: create a story, with characters named entirely differently. The pain then becomes something for your *character* to deal with; the betrayal, the motivation of *their* loved one. Does your perception change when the difficulty is someone else's to face? How big is the problem, really, when it is someone else's?

You may find that, really, the problem is not so very big at all. Even if it is, you know that the characters in your story will find a way to move past it; because they must. So, will, and so must, you.

This is acceptance: acknowledging that a problem is *surpassable*. In doing so, you accept that it happened in the first place, and also that you must work to surpass it.

How to Forgive and, Possibly, Forget

But how in the world do you move past something like a betrayal? How do you rebuild trust? And the question probably forefront on your mind: Why would you want to?

Particularly when it comes to, say, infidelity. Cheating is one of the most heartbreaking difficulties a person can face. It is a betrayal of both the body and the heart, and it shakes a relationship to its core. Insecurity, jealousy, shame—and, of course, a shattered ability to trust the cheater—replace those purer emotions such as affection, respect, and faith.

Infidelity is, therefore, the ultimate test of forgiveness.

Whether or not you believe "once a cheater, always a cheater," it is undeniably true that for some couples, cheating isn't a death sentence. Sometimes, infidelity is really a mistake, a fluke in an otherwise happy relationship.

In such cases, what we need to approach the topic of forgiveness is not judgment, but compassion and communication, and above all an understanding of the importance of trust.

For, again, it is only with trust that we can develop truly fulfilling relationships. It is the cornerstone of, especially, a romantic relationship. When infidelity *is* so common and so often a breaking point in a relationship, the fear of it is extremely powerful in the worst way. Doubt and suspicion can be equally as destructive to a bond as infidelity itself, weakening the relationship before any betrayal has even occurred.

So: to really forgive, you must rebuild trust.

What's needed for both an offering of forgiveness and a renewal trust is above all communication, both with yourself and the other person.

First you must ask yourself: Can I really forgive?

Forgiveness is, above all, unconditional. It doesn't only apply some of the time. Once you've offered it to someone, you can't just take it back. You can't hold a mistake over someone's head as a way to win fights.

It's natural to have leftover feelings, yes. You'll still feel anger, sadness, hurt, and fear, sometimes even years down the line. But you cannot use them against the other person, and you cannot allow them to undo your relationship if you want it to last.

Instead, if committed to forgiveness and to the relationship, you must become committed to radical acceptance and inner peace.

So, can you really forgive? Can you, eventually, be at peace with the betrayal and grow to see the other person not as a villain in your story, but a flawed but well-meaning human, one whom you respect?

If your answer is an honest yes, then you have already begun the hard work. Unfortunately, it only starts here.

After communicating with yourself honestly and openly about what you need and want after a betrayal, you can start the process of doing the same with the other person.

Communication after a betrayal is a challenge, always. The best advice is to establish a safe space, where both of you can express your thoughts and emotions, with no argument. Easier said than done! But to be productive, you must both be willing to be calm and patient.

By agreeing to speak only when the other has finished, to ask tempered questions such as "Why do you say that?" rather than accusations or insults, and by always remembering respect, you can really begin to re-establish a trust between you. Even though they have hurt you, the other person's perspective is important to understand if you wish to rebuild. And it can even be cathartic to lay out all your grievances on the table, to unburden yourself of all the resentment and hurt.

You may have to hold many conversations like this. Overcoming a betrayal isn't possible in a single afternoon, or three. You will have to have difficult conversations and deal with difficult emotions, over and over again.

And communication is only the first step. Those pesky emotions—let yourself feel them, without judgment if you can. Your feelings are only natural. Acknowledge that you have them, but try not to indulge or feed them. Especially rage: feeding anger only strengthens it and makes it harder to move past. When we allow rage to affect our other emotions or even our perceptions, like resentment it warps our interpretation of the situation and alters our ability to adequately face and solve it.

The best way to fight off rage is to above all be intentionally *kind*, not intentionally *right*. When we have been hurt, it is incredibly tempting to lord our victimhood over the one who has hurt us. To hurt them back, in a way, and re-establish our own sense of pride.

But, if you are committed to healing a broken trust, you must find it within yourself to be compassionate. This is not a competition or a game. It is a serious rehabilitation of a relationship. So, just as you accept your own negative emotions, you must also try your best to cultivate more positive ones, such as patience and understanding.

To do this, take breaks from heavy and emotional conversations. You should even take breaks from the person who hurt you altogether if it's getting to be too much. Do some exercises to calm yourself down, such as self-care, meditation, exercise, or talking to an objective third party.

Most importantly: not everything has to be serious. You don't need to have a discussion about the future and the past every time you see the person who hurt you. Try again to reconnect in the ways you first did: watch films, attend concerts, do some silly karaoke. Giggle over work assignments or old photos.

Have fun with each other again. This, above all, will help you to recognize and remember that you are working toward a future, not living in the past.

All of this may seem and indeed be tiring. You may wonder why it's worth the effort, especially when it's not your fault that you were hurt in the first place.

Remember why you want to rebuild trust. You value the other person, in whatever way. They made a mistake, but most likely you know they are more than that. You only need to remember that you do.

If You Struggle to Forgive

Sometimes, if the betrayal cuts particularly deep, forgiveness is an impossible thing to imagine. The idea of it is even laughable. And so, in this section, we focus on forgiveness not as a way to rebuild trust between you and another person, not to save a relationship, but instead as a way to re-establish peace within yourself.

Inner peace is the key to happiness. It is the ultimate acceptance of everything that ever has and ever will happen to you. Many religions, such as Buddhism, extol the virtues of inner peace as enlightenment of the soul. In a chaotic world, it is our most assured chance of contentment.

True happiness, as they say, comes from within.

It may be easier, then, to frame the act of forgiveness as self-care. If you find yourself reluctant to forgive someone because you think they don't deserve it, try to see it instead as a way to soothe all your negative thoughts and emotions about their betrayal.

Pain and rage take up so much energy. It is utterly exhausting to be angry at someone all the time, or to replay their betrayal in your mind over and over again. It's so tempting; we're hurt, we're angry, we have so many things to say and so many questions to ask.

In a way, the pain can even become addictive, a wound we can't stop probing, like a missing tooth we can't stop touching with our tongue. We relive the same disappointment, over and over, until it becomes a habit.

But, if we're being honest, spending hours, days, weeks, or months rehashing the same grievances and arguments will never solve them or make them go away. We all know that, in our hearts.

So, instead, let's view forgiveness not as something you give to someone else, who may deserve it or may not, but as something you give to *yourself*, to heal from heartache.

And, ultimately, as a way to be happy again.

You are, as we'll discuss in the last chapter, your own best ally and friend. Who better to give you happiness than yourself? In forgiving someone who wronged you, you have the chance to become fully self-actualized, confident, independent, and aware of your worth.

You take away the power of their mistakes, and give it back to yourself.

You'll also find that, having found forgiveness within yourself, even if you've not offered it, saying goodbye to the person and the relationship is much easier. Don't feel guilty for having to move on; we must do what is best for ourselves.

Appreciate having had good times with the other person and the chance to cultivate a relationship with them, no matter how long it lasted or how it ended. And then, say goodbye with peace in your heart.

Forgiveness, even if only for your own sake, is the most powerful thing you can do.

Chapter 6:
Trusting After Trauma

Sometimes, though, it can feel impossible to even imagine trusting again; you might find yourself blocking out other people completely instead. Or, you may cling to the idea of trust, in the hopes that it washes everything else away, so much so that you trust those who do not deserve it, or cling too tight even to those who do.

These two feelings may be the result of a deeper trauma: not just infidelity (though that can absolutely be its own trauma), but also something violent or frightening, something which leaves scars.

Trauma can be broadly separated into two categories: collective and individual (Lachmann, 2017, para. 1). Collective trauma refers to events such as experiences of war, a natural disaster, or terrorism. Meanwhile individual trauma is the experience of such things as assault or abuse. It is our lasting, disruptive, often subconscious emotional response to these events which encompass trauma.

Such experiences can be terrifying. They can be life-altering. And so it makes sense that, as a result of their stability and peace being threatened, people who have experienced trauma want above all to feel *safe*.

Safety feels and looks different for different people. Sometimes, safety is precisely what the word itself implies: comfort and protection. Sometimes, however, our idea of safety can in fact adversely affect our relationships with others, and indeed ourselves. It can be counterproductive, even *un*productive.

How do we even begin to move forward in such a case?

Effects of Trauma on Relationships

To better analyze and understand how trauma affects relationships, we'll look first at how it manifests in ourselves and our instincts. Then we will explore how those instincts react when faced with a relationship.

Internal

Traumatized people often face very difficult emotions as a result. They may feel ashamed, alone, anxious, guilty, unlovable, frightened, or even numb. Even worse, they may have trouble expressing any of these feelings.

Depending on the nature of their trauma, they may expect danger or betrayal, and so find it very difficult to trust others. They might go out of their way to avoid conflict, or give in quickly to assumptions of abandonment or rejection; similarly, they may have difficulty believing in another's love, even after multiple reassurances (Brickel, n.d., para. 8). Or traumatized people may feel angry at their own perceived helplessness or lack of control, so in response might try to control others or a situation (ISTSS, 2016, para. 3).

None of these feelings are wrong. None of these reactions are wrong. Our discussion here is never meant to introduce anyone to more feelings of shame, or to feel like they have failed in some way.

Rather, we wish only to introduce the idea of habits and patterns and to give you the tools to recognize them in yourself if they are there, as well as to fix them if need be.

Your trauma is not your fault, nor is how you react to it; but you can absolutely retake charge of your life and of your relationships, even if that trauma is adversely affecting them, even if it feels like an impossible task.

External

So how can trauma affect our relationships?

"Being traumatized is akin to being betrayed" (Lachmann, 2017., para. 6). As we discussed in the previous chapter, betrayal often unearths feelings of shame, hurt, fear, and confusion. This is often how trauma manifests, too. But our reactions to this can differ quite significantly.

Someone who has experienced trauma may approach their relationships in one of two ways: extreme codependency, or extreme mistrust.

In the first instance, we latch onto someone else. We feel frightened and alone, overwhelmed and unstable—so when a friend or a romantic partner offers company, affection, and stability, we cling to that possibility. Essentially, we are trying to heal ourselves via another person.

This approach undermines our relationships in two ways. One, we idolize another person, putting them into a position that is impossible. Lofty expectations, in any relationship, will lead to hefty disappointments. For while our loved ones may comfort and console us, they cannot do our internal work of healing and growth for us.

Inevitably, if we expect anyone to love us perfectly, they will fail.

This is especially true of long-term relationships, because we believe the other person has known us long enough to understand us and help us, in exactly the way we need. So when we feel unfulfilled, abandoned, even rejected—even if the other person has not meant to cause any of those feelings—we blame them. Their inability to be perfect is now their insensitivity. Their failure to heal us is proof of their lack of feeling for us.

And again, even if they convince us again of their love for us, we may place them right back on that pedestal, where they teeter on the edge.

This approach puts enormous pressure on the other person. Our family, our friends, our partners, they do not want to disappoint or hurt us; they want to help us as best they can, and see us happy.

But no matter how much someone loves us, they cannot give us everything we need. The pressure to do so, if they find themselves in that situation, can be utterly overwhelming, and in fact can sabotage the relationship altogether.

When faced with our disappointment and fear—whether a result of trauma or not—the other may begin to feel insufficient, powerless, unappreciated, or even misunderstood themselves. Obviously this puts enormous strain on a relationship, and may fracture it altogether.

This approach also inhibits our own growth, by denying our capability to foster it. When we depend so heavily upon another, when we believe—actively or not—that the love of another will save us, we undermine our own agency, our own strength, and our own courage.

It demonstrates a deep lack of trust in ourselves.

Traumatized people absolutely have the ability to heal. They can do so with the support of their loved ones, and with the guidance of trusted therapists, but any attempts to heal by valuing another more than themselves will inevitably fail.

It is ourselves, our relationship to ourselves, that drives all other relationships. We see the world through how we expect it to treat us, and what we think we deserve. So when we think we deserve the world, we tolerate no less—even of ourselves.

When we expect the world to treat us horribly, of course, we adapt accordingly.

Some, when processing trauma, may resist deep relationships altogether. They may, having faced betrayal, disappointment, abandonment, or rejection, refuse to face such things again, and close themselves off completely.

This, too, is another way to feel safe. Alone, no one can disappoint them. Alone, they cannot feel the pain of being left. Alone, they cannot be hurt.

These people may prefer to handle their struggles themselves, because they do not want to be a burden. They may believe that no one would understand their struggles in the first place, and so refuse to reach out and try. They may believe they don't deserve external support or love at all (Brickel, 2017, para. 5).

This response to trauma, too, demonstrates a lack of trust—this time in others. And perhaps also in ourselves, if we do not believe in our own strength to face pain again, or our courage to be vulnerable, or our worthiness in general.

While very different, these two responses to trauma indicate that trust has been broken, in a deep, profound, and scarring way. Trust in others, in ourselves, in life. But most anything can be repaired.

How to Overcome Trauma and Develop Healthy Bonds

It is the nature of trauma to feel incredibly isolated, to feel like you are trapped behind a wall of pain and fear, and no one can reach you, no matter how loudly you call for help. So you reach out so desperately that perhaps you cling too hard.

It is the nature of trauma, too, to convince us that actually, it's safer behind that wall. Even with all the pain and fear. At least there, no *other* pain and fear can get in. Nothing else can touch us.

These feelings are only natural.

But they are not feelings that have to remain with you for life. No matter how trauma has affected your self-worth or your approach to your relationships, or even your quality of life, there is always a way to emerge from behind that wall.

One way to do this is to take ownership of the feeling completely. To recognize that it is your own; that your memories are your own; no matter how painful or unpleasant, they belong to you and you alone.

This is not a sign that you are, indeed, alone behind that wall with your pain. Rather, it is a healthy and productive reminder that others are often behind their own walls, with their own pain. They may need a little help understanding yours.

Your friends, your parents, even your partner, most likely do not feel what you are feeling. They may not immediately understand. And they will not know, instinctively, exactly what you need them to say and how you need them to act, exactly when you need it. (This applies to any relationship, traumatized or not.)

No, you must help them to feel, understand, and know these things. It may seem exhausting or frightening, and you may wish that you didn't have to explain or ask for help.

But support from others will be so much stronger, and so much more helpful, if you explain the ways in which you need that support.

You must help others to help you.

By doing so, you allow the other person in the relationship to remain fallible, to remain human, even while you give them the tools they need to support you. By acknowledging your own needs and communicating them in a healthy way, you also allow *yourself* the space and opportunity to grow on your own.

If you find the prospect of accepting help, or even cultivating relationships, difficult, try to remember the worthwhile aspects of relationships. The feeling of security that comes with any relationship is attainable.

Be patient with yourself, but also push yourself to test your capability to trust others. Let others prove themselves to you—open a tiny window in the wall, as it were. You may find it's easier said than done. And you may find that you're grateful that you tried.

Even if your worst fears are realized—now you know you are strong enough to overcome them. Even by trying, you've affirmed in your mind that you *are* deserving of stable and fulfilling relationships. You know you can try again.

In both these instances, considering how to strengthen a relationship from a trauma perspective, it's important above all to remember that—as with every problem discussed in this book—communication is crucial. Not just of your own needs, but also of the other person's.

In any relationship, we must recognize the other, but especially in a relationship that needs extra support or care.

Express your gratitude to the other person for their care and affection, and acknowledge their own feelings and perspectives. They might be feeling any number of strange or difficult things, too. There is no suffering competition, even when dealing with trauma; and in a healthy relationship, everyone's feelings are important and valid. Recognize what may be hard or painful for them.

Above all, remember that they are trying, just as you are. Even if it seems effortless for them; even if you think that it should be effortless. Nothing is ever as easy as it seems, for anyone.

Concretely, in this situation it helps to follow our guidelines for healthy communication and boundary setting. Create a sense of safety and stability that surrounds any such discussions or interactions: set a time to talk about heavy topics and a time to not, engage in active listening, and regulate your emotions with breaks.

Also explain if something makes you uncomfortable, or ask for something if you find you need it. Setting boundaries—the guards on your body, thoughts, emotions, privacy, and time—can provide a strong sense of safety if you cultivate them properly around your own comfort and needs.

Both of these practices can help to strengthen our sense of self-worth and to cultivate trust. For more in-depth exploration about boundaries and communication, see chapters 8 and 10.

The work to overcome trauma will not happen overnight; nor is this a comprehensive guide to trauma and relationships. But hopefully, in this chapter, you will have found the encouragement and the opportunity to face these obstacles.

The goal is that this book, as a whole, will provide a framework for developing trust in relationships; no matter what kind, no matter the people in them. Taking it as a whole, and using the lessons from all chapters, will help you to approach relationships with a positive, mindful perspective, one that acknowledges the worth of all people involved. Even when they feel unworthy.

Chapter 7:
Forgiving Yourself

We are, in a sense, the heroes of our own lives. Our lives are stories we live through, day in and day out. Our own perception is the first one we consider, always. Our own choices and actions define our character arcs and our plotlines.

So what do you do if, suddenly, you are no longer a hero—but a villain?

In some ways, forgiving ourselves is even harder than forgiving another person. We cannot escape ourselves, and our minds can be our own worst enemies. Do you ever, in bed at night, remember an embarrassing moment from years ago? High school, perhaps? Even though five or ten or twenty years have passed, the embarrassment is just as sharp and you feel just as squeamish as you did then.

It's just as easy to be unable to forget our mistakes and errors, and just as difficult to shake feelings of shame and guilt. Especially so when the way to overcome these obstacles is not concrete.

As discussed in the previous chapter, forgiveness is an ongoing battle against negativity, doubt, and fear. It is an act and a promise which we must continuously commit to and practice.

Unfortunately for all of us, what this means is that we

cannot just decide to forgive ourselves for a mistake and then instantly forget about it. Our past haunts us. We think of how we hurt our friend's feelings the next time we try to make plans with them; we remember our dissatisfactory performance on a project the next time we go into work.

Even years after we've made such mistakes, at the most random or inconvenient times, we may suddenly recall our very worst moments. Who hasn't laid in bed at night and remembered a time we disappointed our parents, or alienated a friend?

Hurting those we love and respect can fracture our self-image and our confidence. Because not only have we caused pain, we have also discovered or let loose an ugly, shameful side of ourselves. One we never wanted anyone to know about, let alone witness and confront. A side of ourselves that we, ideally, wanted to pretend didn't exist.

No one wants to believe they are the villain of the story. But at some point in their lives, everyone is, simply because they are human.

This chapter deals with the opposite side of the coin than the previous one: how to forgive, rebuild, and move on when *you* are the betrayer. If ever there was a way to learn the humility and compassion needed to forgive someone else, it is the fact that we all, personally, want and deserve it ourselves.

Recognizing Your Own Failure

Before any self-forgiveness can happen, of course, we must acknowledge that we have done wrong in the first place. We must resist denial at all costs. It does neither you nor the other person any favors.

Denial is often a defensive reaction to someone else's anger and hurt. We don't want to believe that we have done any harm, and so we refuse to accept that we did; then the problem becomes theirs. It's *their* fault for overreacting. It's *their* fault for being sensitive.

But convincing yourself—and trying to convince someone else—that you have not made a mistake, or been wrong in any way, is in fact the worst kind of self-sabotage. By doing so, firstly you alienate the other person even more. They will not see you as a friend/lover/coworker who occasionally makes mistakes just like they do; they'll just see a person that they don't really want to know. So, your personal failure becomes the failure of the relationship, and the reason you lose it.

If, at this point, you still deny your wrongdoing, you then enter a vicious cycle, in which you repeat the same mistakes and the same denial patterns. Then you alienate and lose more relationships, because you haven't learned from your mistakes.

Humility is one of the best and most productive emotions anyone can cultivate.

Accepting that we have done wrong is, more than anything, a way to grow and do better in the future. Try saying your mistakes out loud. Tell your reflection in the mirror what you've done. It's awkward, and may be difficult, but by doing so, you acknowledge the situation. You acknowledge that, yes, you have done wrong and how what you've done has affected you and the other person.

And then, you can resolve to do better.

The belief that we can do better is vital to forgiving ourselves. If we believe that we can learn from a bad experience and then never repeat it, that there is hope for us, we can more easily extend compassion and understanding to ourselves for our mistakes.

So, see every mistake, no matter how insignificant or life-changing, as a learning experience—not as a moral condemnation. "I messed up. I may have known better or I may have not, but I did something wrong. Because of the pain I caused and the guilt I feel, though, I know I don't want to make this mistake again. I will be bigger and better than this error of judgment in the future."

Most importantly: "My mistake does not define me."

This is oh-so-hard to believe. Once you have accepted that you've made a mistake, it's a slippery slope to: "I'm a horrible person."

We are hardest on ourselves: our own worst critics. So, personify that critic. Make that negative voice into something separate from yourself. Argue with it! If the negative voice says you don't deserve forgiveness, repeat that you are only human and that you made a mistake, and now you will learn from it.

If it's hard to imagine what to say in response to your inner critic, imagine that instead of speaking to yourself about your mistake, you are speaking to a friend about theirs. Would you say the same things to your friend that you say to yourself? Would you insist that they are not deserving of forgiveness, that they will never be a better person, that everything is ruined for them?

Hopefully, you would never—because those statements simply aren't true.

It's hard to be objective when analyzing ourselves and our lives. But our inner critics are the just embodiments of our most pessimistic thoughts and fears. They are just words we say to ourselves. Simply because we have those thoughts and fears, does not make them true. They are not facts.

They're not necessary, either. Remember that you can silence that inner critic. If you notice that you can't stop thinking about your mistakes, imagine you are stuffing that negative voice into a jar and placing the jar on a shelf. You can open it later, when you're ready and calmer.

But do not let your inner critic destroy your self-esteem and your confidence. Learning and growing from our mistakes means believing in ourselves despite what we have done. If we don't commit to looking towards a bright future, we can't really overcome our past.

In all this time, we haven't yet discussed how to approach getting the other person's forgiveness. Doesn't that affect if we can forgive ourselves or not?

No. It shouldn't, at least. In life, we can control only our own thoughts and actions, good and bad. We can only do things that make ourselves proud or disappoint us, at the end of the day. It's the choice to do either that's important.

Ultimately, self-forgiveness is about your personal healing and growth. It is also the only thing you can control, especially in a relationship which your actions have damaged. You can never decide or control what another person will do about your mistake—only how you yourself learn from it.

How to Rebuild Someone Else's Trust in You

Another key to forgiving yourself for a mistake is by taking positive steps forward. The obvious step is, of course, seeking forgiveness from the other person as well as yourself.

To achieve this goal, healthy and respectful communication is paramount. You've hurt the other person, and the last thing you want to do now is to hurt them more. You must also remember that the other person *does not have to reciprocate*. They are not obligated to listen to or speak with you. So, what you say, and how you say it, must be respectful of their choices and their boundaries.

This is hard to swallow, especially after we have done so much work forgiving ourselves. Now we want the chance to prove that we can do better, since we know ourselves know this to be true. But again, we can't make someone else forgive us or give us another chance. That's up to them and them alone.

So first, make sure that the other person does want to talk. Give them space if they don't, and allow them to set the conversation on their terms if they do. Accommodate the best time and place for *them*. This in and of itself is an apology, a way to say that you respect their hurt and their perspective, and that you appreciate their time.

If the other person has agreed to talk, plan what you're going to say. Make sure that you acknowledge your mistakes, and if they want to know, explain why you did what you did. Also consider how to express that you want the chance to prove yourself to them and to heal as a team. By creating such a plan, your fear of facing the other person and their emotions can be more easily navigated.

It's normal to feel anxious in this kind of situation. Most people hate and fear confrontation, especially when it concerns them and their own actions. And during a confrontation, it's especially normal to feel defensive, or even get our own feelings hurt. The other person might have very complex, difficult emotions, which will affect whatever they say.

Why won't they just forgive us? Can't they see we're sorry? It can be incredibly frustrating.

The best thing you can do to make a difficult conversation a success, or at least the start of one, is just to be patient. The other person is processing their emotions the best they can. Arguing, begging for forgiveness, or airing your own grievances won't fix the situation. Instead, it might make the other person feel pressured, manipulated, or unheard, which will only hurt your relationship even more.

Rather, focus on active listening. Speak not to argue, but to respond. Reply with curiosity and respect; ask 'why' instead of saying 'please.' Acknowledge the other person's feelings and that they have a right to feel them.

Though this may not rebuild trust right away, your willingness to be humble, to show respect, and to listen above all, will demonstrate your commitment to them and to your relationship. It will show that you are prepared to put in the work to make it right.

Again, one conversation most likely won't solve the problem. Hurt, anger, and doubt will resurface, again and again—even your own. When this happens, you must be as patient as possible, and remember that the other person is healing too. If they lash out, it is only a manifestation of their hurt.

It's a complex subject, and you won't always get it right. For more tips on healthy communication, see Chapter 8, "Checking In." Remember that this, like anything else, is a skill. Unfortunately, though, these conversations are only the beginning.

Apologies speak loudly, but actions speak louder. You must do both if you are to regain someone's trust, but you cannot depend on words alone to save your relationship.

To truly repair a relationship that you are responsible for damaging, you must constantly and consciously put in the work. Concrete, consistent action is the best way to re-establish a long-lasting, fulfilling trust.

Now, what 'action' doesn't mean is—for instance—giving your partner access to all of your future text messages, if you have committed infidelity. Personal privacy is a right we all have, regardless of past mistakes. What 'action' does mean, however, is listening to your partner's doubts, fears, and insecurities. It means attending couple's therapy, if that is the right choice for you. It means devoting more time to your relationship, such as organizing date nights or cooking dinner together. It means showing your partner, over and over, that you are devoted to them and that you wish to earn their forgiveness and trust again, and most of all, that you are deserving of it. That they *can* trust you.

It won't happen overnight. They may still feel doubts, insecurities, and anger in a few months, even in a few years. Betrayal, and infidelity in particular, is difficult to overcome—but not impossible.

If you have truly learned from your mistakes, truly forgiven yourself and committed yourself to doing and being better, then this kind of effort will be worth it.

In fact, you may find that such long-term devotion and care will fundamentally change your relationship for the better. Often, in practicing so often to be more respectful, honest, and kind, we adopt those habits permanently.

Even after both of you have healed, the way you treat each other will be, at its core, more loving and more fulfilling. Your relationship won't just be renewed, but strengthened. You will be both less likely to face another betrayal in the future and infinitely better prepared to withstand it.

The dream, right?

Hopefully, if you have done the work to forgive yourself for your own mistake, you do know that to be true: you deserve to be forgiven.

However, despite what you know and believe about yourself, and despite all of your hard work, the other person may not believe you.

They may not want or be able to forgive you.

It's a heartbreaking outcome, especially if indeed you want to work on the relationship and keep that person in your life. If this happens, you may feel angry, confused, or even hurt or betrayed yourself. This is completely natural.

But it is a sign of maturity and growth to remember that, after all, you are the one who has done wrong. Once again, you simply cannot choose how someone else will react to that. It is their right to feel whatever they feel.

We discussed, in the previous chapter, that you are allowed to move on from a relationship if it is no longer working for you. Ultimately, so is a person you've hurt. As much as it makes the guilt and shame of having hurt them even more difficult to bear, it is their choice.

If the other person cannot re-commit themselves to the relationship like you hope they will, focus once more on forgiving yourself. Although it hurts to be rejected, you must not let someone else's reaction dictate your own.

Again, you cannot control the other person's reactions, feelings, or motivations—only your own. So, make them count.

Chapter 8:
Setting Boundaries

Running through previous chapters, but touched on only briefly, is the concept of boundaries. When we talk about respect, healthy communication, and productive action to rebuild a relationship, we're talking about boundaries.

Strictly speaking, a boundary is defined as "something that indicates or fixes a limit or extent" by Merriam-Webster (n.d., a). It's the fence at the end of the lawn or the dotted borderline between countries on the map.

So when we talk about personal boundaries, and specifically about relationship boundaries, we talk about the *limits* and *extents* of what is safe, respectful, or healthy for us. Boundaries provide us with agency— with ownership and control—over our own bodies and emotions, which is vital to cultivating trust.

You see, when we set a boundary in a relationship, and the other person respects our wishes, they show that they care about our feelings and preferences. This builds mutual affection, as well as trust; we know we can depend on the other person, and that above all, we are *safe* with them. And vice versa, of course.

That is trust, at its core: feeling safe, physically, emotionally, and mentally, with someone else.

Boundaries have even more benefits. Creating and

respecting personal boundaries also helps us remember that, though we are in a relationship with another, we are still our own person. Whether it is a romantic or a professional connection, our wants and needs are just as important as those of the other person.

In a healthy relationship, both people are obligated to respect each other's boundaries. Knowing and practicing this reduces the risk of codependency or abuse, as well as the all-too-common over-sacrifice and resulting resentment that many of us experience.

By thinking more in-depth about what makes us comfortable or uncomfortable, we prioritize ourselves in our own lives. Not someone else—ourselves. This can do wonders for our self-esteem, because it reiterates that *we* are important.

It also helps us to view the other person in the relationship more fully, as a fully-fledged person with their own preferences and hang-ups. Our bond with them will be stronger the more we realize this; who doesn't want to more fully understand our friends or our romantic partners?

Recognizing this also makes it easier to, ultimately, practice respect: we want our boundaries treated with care, and we want to treat our loved ones with care in turn.

A relationship with healthy, productive boundaries is more equal, more balanced, happier, and becomes a place for both people to feel safe and respected above all.

So if boundaries are so important and useful, how do we go about creating them?

What Are Healthy Boundaries?

Boundaries are, essentially, our rulebook. They define how we relate to ourselves and the other person in a relationship: what we say and how we say it, how we act, and what our goals are.

We can create boundaries about all kinds of things: our personal space and possessions; the way we approach disagreements and arguments; how often we communicate; our nicknames for each other; the manner of our commitment to each other; and more. And those are just examples for a romantic relationship!

Anything that belongs to you—your voice, your body, your time, your money, your belongings, your emotions, your past, your desires—can be protected by a boundary. So, anything that, by setting limits on, would make you feel happier, safer, or more confident.

These things are, after all, what define you. They, just like you, deserve respect and care, especially by someone who we love, respect, and want to trust.

Keep this in mind, if nothing else because the language of boundary-setting is easily manipulated by those who wish to do so. The opposites of healthy boundaries are as follows: ultimatums, invasions of privacy, or ways to get more attention. Any 'boundary' that infringes upon *another person's* own agency or choice is not a boundary at all but a form of control.

Remember that we set—and follow—boundaries to above all feel freer, more individual, and safer in our relationships.

How to Discover Your Own Boundaries

So: what are our own boundaries?

First, think about what makes you uncomfortable. Don't be surprised if it's difficult! We're so socialized to sacrifice ourselves for the other in a relationship, whether it's romantic or professional.

We have to "pick our battles." We stay silent when our friend wears shoes in our house, even though we have a rule not to, because we don't want to seem rude. We agree to stay late at work because our boss asked us and expected us to, even though we had dinner plans. Our romantic partner walks out of an argument rather than talking through it calmly, like you're trying to.

All of these are examples of boundary-crossing, and all of them are examples of (purposeful or not) disrespect. You don't have to grin and bear these things!

So: what makes you uncomfortable in your relationships? What about how your relationships function, and how the other people in those relationships, does not align with how you'd like to be treated?

Sometimes, we may not even have consciously noticed our discontent. It may manifest in other ways, such as nervous butterflies, or a reluctance to see someone or to go into work.

Pay attention to how you react to people and trust your instincts and your emotions. If you are tense or hurt because of someone's words or behavior, remember that your feelings are important and valid.

Examining these things in turn begs the question of: How *would* you like to be treated?

Would you, in fact, want your friend to wear their shoes inside your house? Would you prefer not to do overtime, and do you want to remind your boss that your free time is your own? Would you want your partner to sit down with you in a heated moment, rather than flee?

What would, above all, make you feel respected and safe?

If you know, it's up to you to explain it.

How to Set Boundaries in a Relationship

As far as we know, no one on Earth is a mind reader. It's counterproductive to be angry or hurt when someone crosses your boundaries if you haven't told them what those boundaries even are.

But when we have previously been self-sacrificial, when we are not used to asking for what we want, the idea of trying to explain and set boundaries with someone is a daunting one.

We don't want to seem needy or rude, presumptuous or overly sensitive. We don't want someone to think we are too much work to handle, or asking for too much. The fear of being perceived negatively, or even worse, of having our requests disdained and refused, can stop us altogether from starting the conversation.

It can be especially difficult in a work environment, where you want above all the trust and approval of your superiors. They do, after all, determine our job security and control our access to greater opportunities. Our bosses are the arbiters of our success, or conversely our failure. No one wants to step on any toes.

But, as in any relationship, disrespect and abuse can happen in a workplace—especially because the power balance is inherently skewed towards the higher-ups. That's why it's even more important to establish boundaries in such a workplace, no matter what those boundaries may be. You should never feel afraid of speaking your mind at your job or of demanding what you are worth.

But how do you go about such a thing?

Again, the answer lies in healthy communication.

In the workplace, for example, the best time to start setting boundaries is as soon as you're hired. If the restaurant manager asks how many hours you want to work, never promise to do more or less than what you're willing to do, simply for the sake of impressing them. If you sign a full-time employment contract, remember that the terms of that contract are negotiable.

Already hired? If you can wait to address your concerns, do so at your next performance assessment. If you don't want to wait, ask your boss to step aside, or whether he has a free moment in his schedule coming up.

Before your conversation, practice what you want to ask for and how you ask for it ahead of time: write it down or speak to your mirror. If you want your boss to stop demanding you respond to work emails over the weekend, prepare a detailed explanation as to why you shouldn't have to.

Try to present that explanation without emotion as best you can, keeping your tone polite and measured. Don't accuse or argue; don't threaten to quit; treat the conversation like a negotiation, and focus on your own perspective.

Make sure you reiterate that this practice, whatever it is, detracts from your happiness with and performance at work—especially if this practice is not part of or goes directly against your contract.

Remember, above all, that your time, your labor, and your comfort is important and worthy of respect.

The same approach applies to friendly or romantic relationships, though perhaps with less formality and care. Let's say, to explore another example, that a close friend constantly makes fun of your outfits. You know they love you otherwise, but their words are starting to get under your skin, and you're starting to enjoy this person's company less and less for fear of what they'll say.

The trick is to use 'I' statements, which lessen the tone of accusation and make the conversation more two-sided and emotive. "*I* feel hurt when you make fun of my clothes, *because* I really like them. If you don't like them, *I'd prefer* that you keep it to yourself in the future."

In emphasizing your own feelings, you validate them both to yourself and to the other person. They should respect your feelings.

The bad news is: sometimes they won't. Be prepared for the other person to take your conversation badly, no matter how fair and justified your points may be or how well you deliver them.

Recognize a negative reaction for what it is: defensiveness. A recurring theme of our book here: no one wants to believe themselves a villain. When people insist they haven't hurt your feelings or disrespected you, they don't want to face the fact that, yes, they have. So, they deny it.

It's a frustrating reaction to encounter. The best thing to do is remain calm and stand by your arguments. Help the other person to understand that you still love and respect them, but that this small aspect of your relationship needs to change for both of you to be happier and healthier.

And if, in the end, they still don't understand, don't be afraid to walk away from the conversation—for now. You have done all this work to discover your own boundaries and even mustered up the courage to set them; don't give up because the other person isn't listening. Instead, be true to your own wants and needs, and try again another time.

If the worst comes to pass, and after multiple attempts the other person still does not understand or attempt to abide by your boundaries, then perhaps it's best to examine whether the relationship is really that fulfilling and meaningful for you.

We all deserve to be in relationships—friendly, romantic, or otherwise—that make us feel appreciated and respected. Any relationship that isn't, is instead a massive drain on our emotional energy, our time, and our confidence. Is a friend who constantly hurts your feelings really that good of a friend? Is a romantic partner who belittles you any chance they get really worth being with?

These are difficult questions, both to ask and to answer.

But the hope is that, having realized you have a right both to your boundaries and to the happiness and safety those boundaries protect, you never settle for less than you're worth.

The Difference Between Secret-Keeping and Privacy

What we must be careful of, however, when setting boundaries, is setting the right ones. Healthy boundaries give us agency over ourselves, our rights, and how much of ourselves we share—or don't.

But what is the line between secret-keeping and privacy?

Imagine you are a teenager again, experiencing all the same emotional highs and lows and all the same drama. You keep a journal, where you talk about your crush, what you want to do with your life, how annoying your younger sibling is. Inside that journal are all your private thoughts, fears, and dreams.

It is, undoubtedly, a cruel invasion of privacy for anyone to read that journal. Despite what some may think, teenagers do have a right to their privacy, and indeed to their freedom. Until mind-reading becomes a known human ability, we all have agency over our thoughts, no matter whether we write them down or not. So, we all have the right to keep the contents of our journals *private*.

However, it would not be right for you, still the same teenager, to deny breaking an expensive vase that you had, in fact, broken. This is secret-keeping.

The difference between them is akin to that of being unobserved versus hiding (Yandura, 2020, para. 8). When we are unobserved, we are free to be ourselves without being watched or judged, having our own singular experiences and thoughts without intrusion. Secret-keeping, on the other hand, is hiding something we are ashamed of or feel guilty about, something we are afraid will hurt or alienate others if they find it out.

As such, secret-keeping is inherently deceitful and dishonest. Privacy is just alone time.

Keep this in mind as you develop and set boundaries with others. Do not let your own boundaries give you a sense of invincibility. While it is undoubtedly an invasion of privacy to go through a partner's texts or emails, don't message someone you shouldn't simply because you know the other person won't find out.

But, you might say, *people do that all the time!*

Yes, unfortunately, infidelity happens all too often. You still shouldn't cross respectful boundaries based on your suspicion. Trust is *never* built on invasions of privacy—if you must go behind someone's back to read their messages, or even demand to see them against that person's will, you simply *do not trust that person*. Your fears and doubts won't go away just because you see nothing suspicious. In such a case, healthy communication and positive action will go much farther.

Additionally, remember that boundaries and privacy are not a shield against pain. Sometimes, we can become so afraid of being hurt that we retreat into our right to privacy, into our own boundaries, so they become a sort of safety net. Walls of stone and brick. Protection against hurt.

But relationships flourish because of intimacy. It's what separates an acquaintance from a best friend. As we'll discuss in the next chapter, don't be afraid of vulnerability, and don't construct your boundaries so tightly that they hide you from the outside world. They're meant to make it easier to see and be seen, based on mutual trust. Which is, after all, the subject of this book!

Chapter 9:
The Necessity of Vulnerability

So, how does vulnerability tie into trust? In essence, they are two sides of the same coin. We trust someone, so we are vulnerable with them. We feel vulnerable, so we want to trust someone. We want someone to know us, so we show them our vulnerability, and as a result, we plant the seeds of trust between us.

The two—trust and vulnerability—cannot exist without each other. They are each dependent on the other to truly succeed and bloom. And where one fails, so does the other.

But vulnerability is, without a doubt, one of the most frightening prospects in a relationship.

Why? Because it is indeed so dependent on trust. If we are afraid to be vulnerable with someone, we are afraid they will react negatively—judge us, mock us, push us away. We don't trust them completely to take care of us. We don't feel completely safe with them.

Yet.

It's natural to want everyone in our lives to see us as powerful and invincible. We want our friends to think of us as effortlessly confident and happy. We want our professors and our bosses to admire our intellect and our work. We want our partners to think compassion, strength, and even love come easily to us, all the time. And we want our children, even, to believe that we are superheroes.

But, as Achilles famously shows us, everyone has a weak spot. There is no shame in it. Anyone worth their salt won't think less of you for having one. Because, trust me, they know they have weak spots too.

And it's the acknowledgment that both of you, that all of us, have weaknesses and flaws, that brings us closer together. It is the act of sharing our weaknesses and flaws with others that makes our relationships into strong, supportive, loving bonds.

But what even is vulnerability, anyway?

Weakness or Strength

Here's the easy answer: it's not kryptonite.

Vulnerability is "the willingness to acknowledge your emotions, even painful ones" (Wignall, 2020, para. 5). In this case, it means to acknowledge those emotions to another, to open your inner world to them. Practicing vulnerability is, as you might guess, at the core of healthy communication.

It's tempting to face and deal with our pain on our own. We so often take on the burden of our own emotions to spare others the effort of carrying them too, and ourselves the humiliation of sharing them.

Surely you know someone who hates to talk about their feelings. Perhaps you even are that person. They rarely confide anything to you about how they're doing, even after an upsetting event such as a breakup or the loss of a loved one. It can be frustrating to watch them go through it alone; all you want to do is help, but you know at the same time that if you try, they'll just push you away.

This is not a statement about how good a friend you are or not. It is, like so many negative reactions we talk about in this book, a defense mechanism.

There is so much pressure on us to be outwardly happy and positive—especially in the digital age, when social media focuses so much on the *highlights* of someone's life, the best moments they can capture and post for likes. We don't see late-night tears on someone's Instagram. We don't see their stress, their fear, their grief, their insecurity. Mostly, we see pretty pictures of brunches, travels, and accomplishments.

It's become a point of pride to project that sort of image to the world—and the worst humiliation and shame to show any other kind of reality, in person or online.

We so often view our negative emotions or experiences as failure. Failure to be happy, to be healthy, to be successful. To be brave, to be productive, to be reasonable. There are so very many ways in which we can fail.

Even worse is the act of sharing our negativity: sharing has become the ultimate failure, because we are not strong enough to deal with these things on our own. Because others now know that we have failed.

Vulnerability has become a weakness.

In fact, it is the opposite.

When we are vulnerable with someone, or even with ourselves, we lessen the power of our fears and doubts. Simply by accepting their existence and sharing them with another, we come to view painful emotions and thoughts as the natural, survivable things that they are. They become easier to face and to overcome.

But when we repress and hide these things, we in fact train ourselves and our brains to believe that emotional pain is dangerous (Wignall, 2020, para. 22). We instinctively avoid any kind of negativity, and so rather than deal with it productively, the emotions mount and mount on top of each other, none of them faced. The anxiety and pressure of carrying those emotions become a thousand times worse than the original negativity was to begin with. Overcoming it all is a herculean task.

Especially when we try to overcome it ourselves. We put immense pressure on ourselves to *just get over it*. Who hasn't said that to themselves after a breakup, sick of missing your ex-partner and wondering what went wrong, if you could have prevented it, what they're doing now? We just want to be *over it*.

To convince ourselves that we are, we go out with our friends. We say "Oh, yeah, I've totally forgotten about him." We even start trying to date other people. All the while we hope no one knows that we cry ourselves to sleep at night.

Unfortunately, we can't flip a switch and stop loving someone just like that, and neither can we stop being hurt that they left as soon as we decide to.

By repeatedly hiding our negative emotions from other people, especially those we should depend on, like our friends, we convince ourselves that we are, indeed, alone with our problems. That we should always be.

More than just to convince others that we are happy and fulfilled, the act of refusing to be vulnerable with another is also meant to spare them the burden of *us*. Our friends don't *really* want to know that we get sad sometimes. They don't want to listen to us complain or vent. They have their own griefs, so how could we ever ask them to deal with ours? Surely they'll love us *more* if we don't depend on them for anything, right?

How to Be Vulnerable in a Relationship

No.

Relationships are, as we said, a mutual knowing. Not just knowing someone's coffee order, or their favorite movie, or their dream job. Not just cheering on their promotions or attending their birthday parties.

To know someone is to see just their pretty sides, but their ugly sides too.

It means witnessing their disappointments, hearing their fears, and commiserating with their anger. It means comforting them through loss and grief. It means helping them to cope with all of this, trying to make them feel better, and, ultimately, cheering them on as they overcome it.

That is the whole of a person: not just their successes, but their failures. In acknowledging and respecting all aspects of someone and their life, pleasant or not, you get to *know* them. And that is all any of us wants, despite the fear of what it means to get there.

Vulnerability is an essential part of caring for each other. By practicing emotional vulnerability, we feel less alone. It is how we *know* we are not alone: we trust another to help us. To keep our secrets safe, to listen to us without judgment, to hope for better with us, and to encourage us to try again.

With the knowledge that we are supported and loved, our confidence, our self-esteem, and our ability to face challenges are all improved and strengthened. We can face anything, knowing that someone we trust is standing at our backs.

As with anything we've discussed here, this is not a quick or easy process. Vulnerability improves trust, but we cannot *really* practice vulnerability without a little bit of trust to begin with.

As we said, the difference between an acquaintance and a best friend is how much you share with them. In the time it takes to move from a stranger to a friend, you start to trust that person instinctively. Simply by spending time with someone and gaining affection for them, trust comes naturally. We want to trust those we care for and laugh with, so we do.

The trick is, obviously, building that tiny kernel of trust into something more.

So, start with the little things. Be vulnerable about your small, everyday sadnesses. If you see a dog walking by that reminds you of your childhood pet, describe how it made you feel. If you got into an argument with your partner, vent about the problem to a new friend. Watch how they react and observe how it makes you feel; were they kind and understanding? Did they help you feel better? If so, they're one to keep.

Next, share your failures. If you are going through a breakup and having a particularly bad day, don't be afraid to say, "I'm really sad today. Can we talk about it?" Chances are they'll happily agree, and not only will they listen and comfort you, but they'll also make you feel better after the fact with wine and a good film.

Because of your respect for each other, and your care and understanding of each other's feelings, you'll feel better and better in each other's company. You'll feel safer. Happier. After a while, that relationship will be so much stronger for it.

The best part is, when we are vulnerable about external things in our lives, such as breakups or firings, we begin to be able to be vulnerable about our deeper emotions, too. The difficult, personal conversations become easier, because we already know that we can trust this person.

We can be vulnerable about insecurities, doubts, and fears. About our need and desire for boundaries, and what those boundaries are. About any difficulties with trust we might have. About everything we've talked about, so far, in this book.

In short, by practicing consistent and healthy emotional vulnerability, we hold the key to strong mutual trust. We hold the key to fulfilling, meaningful, and long-lasting relationships.

And it's no exaggeration to say that without vulnerability and trust, your relationship will not flourish. If you are too afraid to tell a friend or a partner about your feelings, they will feel disconnected from you, and your bond with them will feel stifled, unfulfilling, and lonely. If you feel you cannot confront someone about their betrayal or set a personal boundary with them, because you are afraid of upsetting or hurting them, you'll only become resentful and angry yourself. If you don't even feel comfortable telling someone about a bad day you've experienced, your relationship will cease to be meaningful altogether.

You may as well be alone, at that point.

The relationships you form and keep should enrich your life. Your friends, your partners, and your family—these people's presences in your life should make you happier and give you a sense of belonging. We should never feel lonely in a crowd that we ourselves have chosen.

And those who choose *us* should never feel lonely in our company, either. If we truly commit to being vulnerable in our relationships, we ourselves must commit to helping others be vulnerable, too. Good relationships are a two-way street. An equal exchange. As you become more used to sharing negative parts of yourself and your life, you'll find it becomes easier and easier to do, and the other person, encouraged by your willingness to be vulnerable, will most likely reciprocate.

It can feel awkward, even if we ourselves are used to being vulnerable, to suddenly deal with someone else's sadness and pain. Some people have no idea what to do or say if their friend is crying, for instance.

But it's unfair to expect that others respect your *own* emotional needs if you don't give them the same respect in turn. The lessons here are as much about building others' trust in *you* as they are building your own trust in them. Remember that you want to be someone that others feel they can trust.

Lastly, sometimes, you may find that expressing your own emotional vulnerability—or listening to someone else's—is worse for your mental state than not. It may be that you just don't want to think about your stresses and hurts just then, that you need a distraction.

This is normal and natural. Emotional vulnerability doesn't mean that we must share every little sadness and disappointment in our lives; that would be exhausting! It's simply a way to practice speaking about and confiding more serious things, those things that we have always wanted to say but perhaps never known how to. Things we want to trust people with.

So don't be afraid, and try your hardest, to cultivate relationships that value vulnerability and trust: for both mutual knowing, and mutual happiness.

Chapter 10:
Checking In

After a betrayal, is it really possible to keep the momentum of trust-building going? Can we ever trust that we really know how someone feels? Is there a way to make sure that the relationship—any relationship, even one that is already healthy—is going as smoothly as possible, for all people in it?

Yes, yes, yes!

For all of these questions, the solution is "checking in." But what is that?

Checking in is, in short, making sure that you're on the same page. It doesn't have to be as intense a conversation as the one attempting to reconcile after a betrayal, or the one setting boundaries. It doesn't even have to involve that much emotional vulnerability!

Of course, checking in ties into and helps with all of these kinds of conversations, but really, it comes after the fact. It's the next natural step beyond all the other habits and tips we give in this book for building trust in relationships. Checking in is the *consistent communication* we keep talking about.

Most of our previous chapters have stressed the importance of communication to building trust. But for many of us, just opening our mouths and speaking seems daunting, especially when we have to talk about something very personal, something that causes us pain or grief. It's easy to say, "Use 'I' statements" and "Be emotionally vulnerable," but how, really, do we create an environment in which we can do that?

In this chapter, first we'll explore more ground rules for healthy communication, in all situations and for all reasons. Then we'll discuss more in-depth the concept of "checking in," and how to make it a natural, integral habit that happens, nearly, on its own.

Because of how often people stress the idea of healthy communication, we can get an idea of it as a very serious, long-winded conversation, which we have to have every day in order to be really *healthy*. That's not the case. In fact, one can argue that this idea creates too much pressure to be healthy at all.

With checking in as an instinctive habit, however, the need for serious, long-winded conversations can all but disappear. Checking in is all about making sure the other person is happy, and believing their answers. It is about cultivating demeanors and behaviors that allow for honest, simple communication with no fuss. It is, as always, about trust.

Deliberate Communication

Before we really discuss checking in, though, we have to learn the basic principles of healthy communication.

The more serious, involved conversations that we talked about are all about being the most productive and respectful we can, while minimizing emotional overload or stress. The kind of communication that builds trust and supports fulfilling connections is not accompanied by the sound of shouting. It is not dramatized by tears.

Instead, it is empathetic and engaged, with no ulterior motives except to more fully understand the other person and to connect with them in a stronger way. And it is conducted in an environment that encourages all of these things.

The first step to creating that environment is, of course, to be in person. It may seem obvious, but with the advent of the Internet and especially of cell phones, we can be tempted to have serious conversations over text. It's less awkward for us; we don't have to worry about eye contact, tears, or raised voices. We have more time to think about our responses and theirs, and we don't have to face rejection head-on.

But text communication is flawed in fundamental ways. Text messages just consist of letters on a screen; there is no nuance or tone to the words. Our interpretation of those words can differ vastly from the way in which the other person meant them. It's so easy to project our own insecurities and doubts onto stray words, an ambiguous phrase, or even a period. Does that sound healthy?

Similarly, as we'll discuss in the next few pages, body language is a crucial part of communicating with others. It's the undercurrent of and punctuation to our words;

it can bring us much closer to understanding each other. Without it, our conversations miss something essential. Phone conversations lack this as well as text exchanges, so they too should be avoided, even though we can hear inflections in the other person's voice over the phone.

Face-to-face communication, as frightening and intense as it can be, is really the best way to reach each other across the divides of our own emotions and perspectives.

And make sure to pick a good time for the discussion. Don't surprise the other person; if anything, agree on a good time to talk beforehand. The last thing anyone wants is to hold a heavy conversation when they thought they'd just be watching a film, or when they are in the middle of an important task. By planning ahead, you reduce stress on both sides and allow you both to prepare what you want to say.

Another way to make these conversations more productive is to practice active, engaged listening: approaching the conversation not with the intent to speak but to *listen*. Not waiting for the other person to finish speaking so you can talk about your own perspective, but responding to *theirs* after they're done.

Simply by listening to someone's voice in a more meaningful way, by hearing their emotions in their voice, you can understand their perspective and their approach to the conversation better. You'll respond not only to their words but also to their emotions, which will help balance the conversation (Robinson, 2019, para. 9).

So, how do we practice active, engaged listening?

Limit distractions. Don't try to have the conversation in public, like at a coffee shop for example. Don't check your phone. Don't try to talk during a film or anything similar. The conversation should be between the two of you alone, and the person to whom you're speaking deserves your full attention. Ask that they, too, respect this rule if you find that they aren't paying much attention.

Again, don't just wait for them to finish speaking so that you can speak. And don't interrupt! The trope of a "talking stick" is, really, a good one, in that it emphasizes the importance of giving everyone their moment to talk and be heard. If you don't want to be that cheesy, just remember to take the conversation in a slow and measured way. There's no rush.

Focus on your empathy and your curiosity—not on your anger or your sadness. Often, a difficult conversation that emphasizes honesty can bring up hard topics. What other people feel and haven't before shared can really surprise us. Try not to give in to your defensiveness or hurt.

A good way to do this is, again, to slow the conversation down. If our partner says, for example, that they think we dismiss their emotions, don't reply with "I don't do that!" Ask instead, "Why do you feel that way?" or "What do you mean?" Respond with the intent to *understand*, not to *argue*. Healthy conversations are not about winning, but about connecting more deeply.

And when you have the chance, you can express your own feelings, but remember not to accuse. Don't do name-calling. Say instead things like, "When you do *this*, I feel *this way.*" Remember our lessons from the chapters about forgiveness and emotional vulnerability.

Additionally, engaged listening, and honesty, are strengthened—or undermined—by body language. If you are in person having this conversation (as you should be), be mindful of how you are expressing your thoughts and emotions through your body. As social animals, we are skilled at reading each other through facial expressions, hand gestures, and postures. Even if we only notice these things subconsciously, they can have a profound effect on the success of any conversation.

When the other person is speaking, be sure to visually encourage them. Nod to show them you are listening, smile when you make eye contact. Make sure your posture is open: don't cross your arms or turn your body away. Don't shake your head. This could make you come across as dishonest (Robinson, 2019, para. 24). Rather, arrange your position so that you seem welcoming and patient; the other person will register your body language and react accordingly. It's just one way to make the conversation run smoothly.

Speaking of calm: pay attention to your stress levels and theirs. Conversations, no matter the topic or the people holding them, can get emotional, and when serious discussions are overwhelmed by intense emotions, they can quickly go off the rails and become unproductive.

Give yourself time to answer and respond. Even though you are face-to-face, there's no pressure to reply as soon as the other person has finished speaking. Focus on your thoughts and arrange them as best you can before you speak. In that pause, too, you can soothe your own emotions: take deep breaths, or focus on a sight or a taste.

If either of you feel too overwhelmed to continue just then, don't hesitate to ask for a break. These kinds of conversations can take a long time to reach their natural conclusion. Take a moment to yourself. Go to the bathroom, go for a walk, or stop to eat. And you don't have to come back to it that day, either. Agree to pause and pick up the conversation again the next day, or even the next week.

Of course, a great way to break the tension is to look for humor. Don't crack jokes at anyone's expense— unless you're comfortable making fun of yourself—but look for some small ways in which you can see a lighter version of events. It can even be something that's completely unrelated to the topic at hand! Laughter is a great stress-reliever, as well as a way to remember that, even though you may be finding it difficult to speak to each other or to see eye-to-eye right now, you are allies. You're putting in all this effort to take extra care because you are, at heart, on the same side.

The point of healthy communication is to bring people into a deeper understanding of each other. There are many ways to do this, and the emphasis should always be on respect and compassion, both for yourself and for the other person.

Following these tips is meant to create an environment in which trust can bloom, through people speaking honestly and freely, without fear of judgment.

Natural, Daily Communication

If serious conversations or topics make you uncomfortable, even after all these helpful tips, the good news is that once a relationship is truly strong and full of trust, the need for those kinds of conversations disappears.

Often, we have to hold these kinds of formal discussions when something is wrong. When someone has made a mistake, or when a relationship simply isn't working as well as it could be.

But by using the tools and concepts we've discussed here, trust and respect will build, and there won't be so much to fix or address. Think of mutual forgiveness, positive action, boundary-setting, and emotional vulnerability as bricks to build a wall around your bond, keeping awkwardness, distrust, anger, and resentment at bay.

And add to those tools another one: checking in. This is an adaptation of the more formal way of communicating that we discussed in the previous section. After a distance between two people has been crossed, and as their relationship begins to grow and mend, they can trust themselves and each other to say just as much, but faster, easier, and with much less pressure.

What this means is making asking the other person how they are a daily habit, and creating an environment in which they, and we, can be honest and open, without fear of judgment or real confrontation.

So, asking "How are you feeling?" becomes a genuine question, not one asked for the sake of politeness but to get a real answer with which we will deal fairly. "How did you feel when I did this?" "Do you like it when I do this?" These questions show that we respect the other person's feelings and want to take care of them, especially when we respond positively.

That's the trick: making sure the other person knows, always, that what they say will be respected and considered. Getting angry, denying their feelings, refusing to change, dwelling on our own mistakes—you must follow the steps to moderate your own emotional response and take care to see any negative thoughts or emotions as simply a puzzle to work out *together*, not an accusation.

Additionally, when we ourselves feel uncertain or uncomfortable about something, getting into the habit of simply saying, "Can you do/not do this? It made me feel weird," is a good way to become more assertive and more direct in our relationships. By expressing our feelings and not hiding or suppressing them for the sake of politeness or avoidance, not only do we create an environment of respect, we validate our own right to our feelings and to our happiness. When we believe that we have the right to take up space and ask for what we want, our self-esteem skyrockets.

The more we practice asking and answering these questions, the more normalized it will become to tell each other our thoughts, and not to bottle up our hurts or resentments. Problems are discussed and dealt with before they turn into anything heavier or more serious. No more expecting the other person to read our minds; no more silent suffering. No more discontentment that causes bigger and deeper problems.

Plus, the better we get at checking in, the less formal it has to be. Unlike the more intense kind of conversation we discussed earlier, this kind of practice could even be conducted over text. Consistent, intentional practice will turn checking in into a natural habit, one we don't even have to think about.

The most important thing to take away from this section is that our questions, and our answers, to each other have to be honest and meaningful. This kind of practice can't just be performed for appearances. It must be genuine, just as we want our relationships to be genuine.

Even with such a simple question as "How are you?", respect and care of each other's feelings, healthy communication, and above all trust, will become so much a part of how we treat each other that there will be no room for doubt or fear.

Chapter 11:

Your Relationship with Yourself

Throughout this book, we've touched on the importance of affirming yourself and making sure your relationships are equal and balanced, favoring neither one person nor the other. Now, in this last chapter, we'll focus on the most important—and often the most neglected—relationship in any of our lives: the one we have with ourselves.

Why the most important?

Because, as I said earlier in the book, we are with ourselves always. We cannot slowly drift away from ourselves, as with friends; we can't quit ourselves, like we do with a job; we can't break up with ourselves and later on fall in love with a new self in a different city. In every waking moment, and even while asleep, our closest companion—or enemy, or both—is ourselves.

We are always at the mercy of our own thoughts, wants, fears, regrets, doubts, and insecurities. Indeed for many, their minds can work against them, with illnesses such as anxiety or depression, which can profoundly affect our self-esteem, our confidence, our happiness, and even our success in life.

Additionally, because we are always inside our own heads, we don't always see ourselves and our actions objectively, or even the way others, with their own perceptions, would. Our own selves, as well as the world at large, are always colored by our biases.

It's exhausting to think about, isn't it?

Given how closely ourselves and our ideas of self, our thoughts and our emotions, are intertwined, it's incredibly easy to forget about ourselves altogether. To forget that, even if we were the last person on earth, we would still have one relationship: the one with ourselves. As long as we live, we will have a relationship with ourselves. One that deserves and needs the same attention, care, and commitment as any other.

It's up to us, ultimately, to make that relationship as healthy and productive as it can be. No one else can put in the work for us. When we are lonely, it's so easy to fall into the trap of believing that a new friend, a better job, or the next lover will make us truly happy, affirm our worth forever, and help us feel beautiful.

The grass is always greener, as they say. But depending on others to improve our own self-esteem is a dangerous, slippery slope. We must take responsibility for our own inner peace and contentment, to the best of our ability.

Doing this won't help just us. By following steps that help us to realize our own importance and worth, and by being consistently kind and compassionate towards ourselves, our relationships with others will become easier, too.

We won't be so afraid of vulnerability. We won't

hesitate to ask for respectful boundaries. We'll be more vocal and confident during our hard conversations.

Confrontation, or even rejection, won't devastate us so badly, because we'll know that we can get through it, and that we deserve better—that a betrayal of us is never our fault.

The idea of trusting someone else will stop scaring us so much.

In short, our relationship with ourselves can strengthen and enrich every single other relationship we have. So, why not make it the best we possibly can?

Recognizing Your Own Worth

Before we begin, a disclaimer: that popular saying that you can't really love anyone until you love yourself? That is simply not true. Everyone is deserving and capable of love, regardless of whether they have poor self-esteem or not. By saying such a thing, and by perpetuating such an idea, we stigmatize those who suffer from mental illness especially. We often make their self-worth even worse, by telling them that unless they are perfect, they will never be happy.

Belief in this idea drives people to think that their own view of themselves is objectively true and that everyone else sees them that way too. They then accept unhealthy relationships, because they believe they don't *deserve* to be treated well.

This is absolutely wrong.

No one is perfect. No one will ever, truly and completely, love themselves. We all struggle with our own faults and mistakes. We all wish we were better. We all look at other people and wish we were more like them: better looking, smarter, more driven, funnier—anything others have that we think we lack, we want and blame ourselves for *not* having.

However, as we said, because we're so tied to our own thoughts and perceptions, it can be impossible to see ourselves clearly. Just as you can't understand a painting if you only look at its bottom right corner, or a book if you read just a single page. We are all more complex than our flaws; it's just hard to remember when our flaws are all we can focus on.

Confronting Our Own Thoughts

Often, our negative thoughts can become addictive. We dwell and dwell, making ourselves feel worse and worse. In some way, perhaps we think we deserve it. Especially when we are thinking of our own mistakes, or how much we wish we were someone else entirely.

And these thoughts have a way of snowballing, growing bigger and uglier, until they are all we can see, all we can think, and all we can believe. The stray thought that our coworker is very talented can become the thought that we are not as smart as they are, which can become the thought that we don't deserve the promotion coming up that we've been working so hard for, which can become the thought that we will never succeed in life, and so on and so on.

It's a vicious cycle from which we all suffer, and which we all find difficult to escape.

One way to stop it, however, is simply to notice that you are having these thoughts. Often we don't even notice our negativity towards ourselves. Have you ever looked in a mirror and critiqued your own appearance before you even consciously realized you were doing it? It's almost an instinct. We say something negative about ourselves, without even questioning it, and then we move on with our day, feeling just a little bit worse.

But even by just being more aware of our negativity, we challenge them. Keep a tally in the notes app on your phone of all the times you accuse yourself of inadequacy or failure. The number alone should shock you and make you realize that the way you think about and talk to yourself is neither fair nor kind.

Pay attention, too, to the structures of these negative thoughts. Are you downplaying your achievements by turning your positives into negatives? Saying, "They're only my friend because they feel bad for me?" Or are you seeing everything in black and white, all-or-nothing? "If I don't get this job, I'll never succeed in my career."

Notice, above all, if you mistake feelings for facts. Everyone does this, and it's the hardest thing to confront and disbelieve. For example, say you notice that your partner has been distant lately. You worry that means they are falling out of love with you. The more attention and energy we give to this thought, the more we believe it, until we are convinced that our partner wants to break up with us and expect it at any moment.

But it is only our emotions—our doubts and our fears—that have made us believe that, not any kind of evidence other than the fact that they have been distant. This could be due to any number of things, most of which have nothing to do with us.

These are all examples of negative thought patterns that, really, we don't even recognize. By giving a name to this kind of thought structure, it becomes easier to realize that our negativity is affecting and even controlling the way we see ourselves and the world around us.

Once you begin to pay more attention to your negativity, it then becomes easier to adjust and re-route those kinds of thoughts. Rather than focus on your faults, try to see your strengths, and what you've learned from your mistakes. "Yes, I made a mistake in *that* way, but I succeeded in *this* way." Turn a negative into a positive, instead of the other way around. The trick is not to dwell, but to accept your negative thoughts and then to make your positive thoughts more powerful.

It may help, too, to imagine that you are speaking to someone else instead of yourself. Would you speak to your best friend in the same way you speak to yourself? About their personality, their achievements, even their appearance? No! You would comfort them, lift them up, and distract them. You are no less deserving of compassion than they are, just because you are you.

Speaking of distraction: another trick to stop negative thoughts in their tracks is to focus the mind on something else completely. Do a sudoku puzzle or a crossword; solve a complicated math problem; practice an instrument or start cooking a complicated meal. The new challenge will distract you from the negative thoughts and reset your brain (Cirino, 2018, para. 11).

Now, this is by no means a definitive guide to negative thoughts or self-perceptions. These tips are a good starting point for changing thought patterns, but they will be not easy or even completely possible for some people.

No matter how easy or how difficult, the journey of improving our relationship with ourselves doesn't have to be undertaken alone.

There is no shame in seeking out help from a professional. Therapy is an incredibly helpful tool, no matter whether you suffer from occasional low self-esteem or from extremely difficult mental illness. A good therapist will help you to examine and improve all your relationships, not just the one with yourself, and will help and encourage you to succeed and thrive. Attending therapy says nothing about your strength or your weakness, only the simple fact that you are improving your own mindset with the help of trained guidance.

Me, Myself, and I

Beyond changing thought patterns, though, there are more habits and practices that we can adopt to improve our self-image and our relationships with ourselves: proactive, positive actions that, over time, will help us to have more belief and trust in our own value and abilities.

We can divide these habits into two categories: self-care, and self-dating.

Self-Care

Self-care is simply that: taking care of ourselves. This can include basic things such as personal hygiene and nutrition, but here we're going to focus on the more mental and emotional aspects of self-care.

It's all about giving ourselves and our emotions space and attention, and doing things to make ourselves happier or more stable. It isn't always fun or easy. Bubble baths, comfort films, and soothing music are certainly aspects of self-care that can help us calm down and feel safe, but there is much, much more to it.

One place to start is keeping a journal. This practice has several pros. By writing down our thoughts, we separate them from ourselves, in a way; much like confiding in someone else, the weight of our worries and hurts becomes less heavy just by setting them to paper. Also, by organizing them in such a way, we can analyze and work through our thoughts and emotions much better. Those negative thought patterns we talked about earlier become easier to spot and to unravel. We can recognize our own blind spots and misconceptions.

Meditation can also help in this way. Daily meditations can promote mindfulness, which helps to reduce worry and fear and to keep us in the present moment. Meditation teaches how to accept thoughts and how to let them go, whether they are incredibly happy or incredibly negative. This can greatly lower our stress levels and help us to keep problems in perspective.

Another mental self-care practice is daily affirmations. These are short sayings that we repeat to ourselves to validate our own self-worth and ability. We believe what we think. By repeating positive thoughts, especially over negative thoughts, we train ourselves to believe them. Affirmations can be anything, like "I am beautiful" to "I deserve to be happy," but they should above all *affirm* our value as human beings.

The last self-care practice is more practical: social media detoxes. As the world becomes more and more digital, we show more and more of our achievements and successes online. Even if we don't realize it, we all fall into the trap of believing that what others post on social media reflects their entire life—that they wear those smiles all day, that they succeed at everything, that their relationships are perfect. We judge and compare and nearly always find ourselves wanting, even for the number of likes we get! But these things just don't reflect real life; and no one can lead a fulfilling life completely online. The best thing to do to protect ourselves from this is to take regular social media breaks. Even just a day away from scrolling can be beneficial and remind us that, at the end of the day, our own happiness is the most important thing.

That is the goal of all these habits: improving our own happiness. They may seem like more effort than they are worth, but like with any skill, after some practice these self-care tools become easier, and, ultimately, improve our lives.

Self-Dating

A more fun way to improve our relationships with ourselves is to see them as just that: relationships. And what do you do in a relationship? You hang out! You enjoy each other's company! Why not do the same with yourself, both to have fun and to improve yourself?

There are so many activities that you can do to build your own self-esteem while enriching your life at the same time.

A great example is volunteering. Giving back to the community can vastly improve our own self-worth, for the simple fact that when we help others, we feel better. Knowing that you have helped someone in some small way, even if just by putting a smile on their face, is one of the best feelings in the world. Additionally, volunteering puts our own troubles into perspective, further lowering our stress levels.

On a more personal level, hobbies are crucial to developing a relationship with ourselves. Picking up a new hobby can be an incredible challenge and unexpected joy. Simply by developing more interests, you have more to focus on—and less time to devote to negative thoughts—and you gain a deeper, richer sense of self. You surprise yourself, you become more unique and interesting, and you depend less on others to entertain or distract you.

You'll find that this, in turn, strengthens your other relationships, giving you more confidence as well as more to talk about and share with friends and partners.

From there, it becomes less bizarre—and less daunting—to consider the idea of going on self-dates. Yes, dates with yourself. Say you are learning to play piano. Why not go listen to a concert? Or you're a foodie; attend a cooking class. You love history, so watch a reenactment! The list goes on and on. The more comfortable you are in your own company, the easier it becomes to, say, eat dinner at a restaurant alone, to see a film or a play by yourself, or to walk through a museum on your own.

This isn't the behavior of a lonely person. Rather, it shows someone who is comfortable being alone, who is confident being alone, and who enjoys life no matter who they are with. Once you become comfortable 'dating' yourself, you truly become self-dependent, someone who knows they can heal from the loss of any other relationship.

All of this, from self-care to self-dating, is meant to help you develop a positive sense of self that is separate from anyone else. By practicing self-care, you acknowledge the importance of your thoughts and emotions; by filling your time with productive activity and pursuing personal interests, you enrich your own experience of life and your confidence.

This is your relationship with *yourself*, after all.

Demanding What You Need and Want

And when it comes to how that relationship affects all our other ones, a more positive self-image will absolutely result in a more positive interpersonal connection. Simply the belief that we ourselves have value will lead us to expect that others believe the same, and act accordingly.

In the same vein, any betrayal, any rejection, that diminishes our value won't be as devastating. As we said above, practices such as self-care and self-dating help to increase our dependency on ourselves and our own abilities, and to see more value in ourselves. As such, we will stop searching for and indeed craving someone else's good opinion of us. We will stop needing others to affirm our value for us.

This is incredibly important, as it can reduce the risk of codependency. Your self-worth should be wrapped up in your own *self*—not in someone else's idea of you. Such dependence on someone else, especially when it comes to self-esteem and confidence, is very dangerous; that person could, at any moment, destroy our self-image and tie it to themselves, making that relationship unequal and unhealthy. No matter how much you trust someone, you must maintain healthy boundaries with them: dependency of self is one of those boundaries.

When we realize that our happiness and our confidence can come from within ourselves, as we learn when we practice mental self-care and develop our own hobbies, our other relationships are not so integral to our identities.

It then becomes easier to practice everything else in this book: boundary-setting, emotional vulnerability, healthy communication, even forgiveness. When we believe in, trust, and love ourselves, we don't simply want good relationships; we expect them. We demand them.

We build them.

Conclusion

So. Here we are, at the end of the book. Hopefully, by now, you have learned a lot about relationships, about trust, and about yourself. Hopefully, it wasn't too preachy! All of the lessons, all of the tips, all of the tools: they are meant only to help, guide, and comfort you as you navigate the treacherous waters of human relationships.

Creating and keeping meaningful, healthy bonds with other people isn't easy. If it were, books like this wouldn't exist. (What would we do without self-help?) We don't naturally understand how to be emotionally vulnerable, how to be good communicators, or even how to gain confidence in ourselves. We aren't born knowing the best ways to set personal boundaries, or that we can even *do* such a thing.

There's no shame in any of that. Though some argue that there is a set, objective morality system that all humans understand from birth, it isn't always clear what is right and what is wrong. Especially when feelings are involved. *Especially* when one of those feelings is love.

Our relationships with other people are (mostly) defined by love. We want to love our family, our friends, and most of all our romantic partners. We long for love, we dream of it, and we try our best to make it last when we find it.

But sometimes, love is overshadowed by other, more negative things: insecurities, doubts, and fears. Anger, suspicion, and resentment. Sadness and pain. Indifference, misunderstanding, and cruelty.

Betrayal.

Distrust.

Even hatred.

Some of these emotions are normal. But most of them are unnecessary, and none of them whatsoever have to mean the end of a relationship.

Having the right relationship with *yourself* is the first and the best way to understand, create, and maintain any other. It's easier said than done, and of course it's not a necessary prerequisite to being loved by anyone else; anyone can have good relationships, regardless of whether or not they love themselves perfectly and take care of themselves every day.

It doesn't have to be perfect. It doesn't have to be every day. That wouldn't be possible anyway, for anyone. But even just by trying to believe in ourselves, we acknowledge the fact that we are deserving and worthy, both of someone else's love and of our own.

Out of all the relationships we encounter in life, the one we have with ourselves is the most difficult: the most dramatic, the most suffocating, and the most critical. But, like any other relationship, it can get better. Confronting our own negativity and cultivating our own interests helps us to live happier, stable, and enriched lives, all on our own.

Committing to improving our relationships with ourselves also helps us to realize that our connections with other people should make our lives better, too. Knowing how to ask for this, and even what to ask, is only one step of many to creating relationships founded on trust.

Of all the obstacles to happy, healthy relationships, trust is the biggest and most difficult one to face. We all struggle with it. It's hard to quantify, and even harder to keep up, especially when something threatens it. Even if you do trust someone completely, some days you might not. Some days you won't trust anyone in your life, not even yourself.

But without trust, there really can be no love or respect. A relationship without trust is always unstable and always in question. To use the old adage, it's a house built on sand. Standing inside it, we might feel anxious, queasy, and afraid. We might be afraid to move around or step out. We might wonder why in the world we built this house at all. And even when we build a different house, we might worry that it, too, is built on sand, even if we didn't see any.

So there we start: by asking. Is this house built on sand? If so, what can we do to save it?

Unfortunately, most of the time, you can't fix it in just one go. Trust is not constant. It requires work.

Healthy communication is just one aspect of that work. Actively, honestly, and respectfully expressing our own thoughts and emotions, and listening to those of others. It's through really speaking our minds and listening to each other that trust has a true chance to thrive, and it's a lack of productive communication that often signals a problem in a relationship.

We bottle up our fear that our friend dislikes us and just take what they give. We argue with our boss more than we compromise with them. We don't like the way our mother criticizes our weight gain, so we get impatient and snap at her. We suspect our partner of cheating, so we spend less and less time with them, just in case.

When confronting these problems and these people, sometimes we blow up or we cry. We let ourselves become twisted with self-righteousness, resentment, and self-pity. We reduce the other person, or ourselves, to villains and enemies.

Or we just accept the state of affairs, cycling through the same negative and unproductive patterns again and again, because they're all we know. Because we think relationships can't really *involve* trust, or that we just don't deserve to have one like that.

This is not the way it has to be. If there is anything this book should have taught you, it is that you can always demand better.

Even if you have never had it before. Even if trauma wants to make you believe that it is unattainable.

But what's better? *Better* is healthy boundaries that determine our comfort, our emotions, and our privacy, protecting our independence and our feelings of safety. *Better* is true emotional intimacy, nurturing our closeness with others and our confidence that we are loved. *Better* is the strength to accept pain and guilt, and the courage to forgive, if not for others then for ourselves.

It's the courage and, above all, the tools, to prepare us for that most difficult of relationship challenges: betrayal.

Betrayal will happen. No matter how strong a trust between two people is, no matter how deeply they love and respect each other. At some point, they will hurt each other. It's just a natural part of being human, and so being imperfect.

Whatever form this betrayal takes, it will no doubt be painful. It may even shake you to your core. But hopefully, this book will have taught you too that a betrayal is not the end of the world, or even the end of a relationship. It is only a setback. It may even be a minor one.

The lessons in this book won't work for everyone, every relationship, or every situation. You may refuse to try or use some of the suggestions here, or even flat out disagree with them! But any of them, or all of them used together, can fundamentally change the way you approach your relationships and yourself.

Each tool and habit, from forgiveness to self-dating to understanding different relationship expectations, informs and strengthens the others. For some, emotional vulnerability sounds like a nightmare; but learning how to lessen the stress of serious conversations can make the idea a little easier. For others, learning to recognize the various indications of disillusionment or unhappiness in their relationship can help them understand exactly how to set new boundaries. Still others may feel enlightened after reading about attachment styles and feel that so many habits and frustrations have been explained.

But above all, healthy and trusting relationships need the people in them to believe that they are worthwhile. No amount of communication tips or new boundaries can make you believe in that.

After all, relationships are beautiful. We all want good family bonds that support us through life and help us to belong. We all want friends who make us laugh. And who doesn't long for a great love, the kind you read about in books, the kind that lasts for whole lifetimes? Or, more practically, who doesn't hope for a respectful, fair boss and capable coworkers?

Even after disappointment and loss, most of us still want to build new relationships, better than the last, closer and more fulfilling. Despite how difficult it is to trust, we try, and try again. We hope that this time, it will be different. And if we can't hope for that, we mourn the fact that we can't. Because in the end, relationships are better than being alone.

But relationships can be more than just *not being alone*. Every relationship we have, every bond we create, can be more than that. The horror of discovering that our trust in someone, or someone else's trust in us, was misplaced just doesn't have to happen again—or at least, it can be faced with confidence, with determination, and with grace.

Imagine this. Founded on trust, bound by emotional vulnerability, strengthened by healthy communication, and protected with our own self-worth, our relationships will be about being *together*. Now, isn't that a fantastic idea?

References

Brickel, R.E. (2017, Sep. 15). *3 Concepts to Help Trauma Survivors Move Forward Into Healthier Relationships.* Brickel and Associates. https://brickelandassociates.com/healing-relationship-trust-after-trauma/

Brickel, R.E. (n.d.). *Loving a Trauma Survivor: Understanding Childhood Trauma's Impact on Relationships.* PsychAlive. https://www.psychalive.org/loving-trauma-survivor-understanding-childhood-traumas-impact-relationships/

Chesak, J. (2018, December 10). *The No BS Guide to Protecting Your Emotional Space.* Healthline. https://www.healthline.com/health/mental-health/set-boundaries

Cirino, E. (2018, May 24). *10 Tips to Help You Stop Ruminating.* Healthline. https://www.healthline.com/health/how-to-stop-ruminating

Couples Academy. (2018, February 5). *It's A Thin Between Privacy & Secrecy.* Couples Academy. https://couplesacademy.org/2018/02/05/its-a-thin-between-privacy-secrecy/

International Society for Traumatic Stress Studies. (2016). *Trauma and Relationships.* ISTSS.

https://istss.org/ISTSS_Main/media/Docume
nts/ISTSS_TraumaAndRelationships_FNL.pdf

Lachmann, S. (2017, April 10). *When Trauma Affects Your Trust in Your Relationship*. Psychology Today. https://www.psychologytoday.com/us/blog/m e-we/201704/when-trauma-affects-your-trust-in-your-relationship#:~:text=When%20you've%20endu red%20collective,or%20not%20one%20will%2 0follow

Lindberg, S. (2018, July 24). *12 Tips for Forgiving Yourself*. Healthline. https://www.healthline.com/health/how-to-forgive-yourself

Mateo, A. (2019, August 21). *Signs You Might Be in an Unhappy Relationship*. Oprah Magazine. https://www.oprahmag.com/life/relationships-love/a28725954/signs-of-unhappy-relationship/

Mayo Clinic. (2017). *7 steps to boost your self-esteem*. Mayo Clinic. https://www.mayoclinic.org/healthy-lifestyle/adult-health/in-depth/self-esteem/art-20045374

Merriam-Webster. (n.d., a). Boundary. In *Merriam-Webster*. https://www.merriam-webster.com/dictionary/boundary

Merriam-Webster. (n.d., b). Confidence. In *Merriam-Webster*. https://www.merriam-webster.com/dictionary/confidence

Merriam-Webster. (n.d., c). Trust. In *Merriam-Webster*.
https://www.merriam-
webster.com/dictionary/trust

Newsome, T. (2016, January 8). *9 Boundaries You Need
To Set Up In Your Relationship*. Bustle.
https://www.bustle.com/articles/133438-9-
boundaries-you-need-to-set-up-in-your-
relationship

Robinson, L. (2019, March 21). *Effective Communication*.
HelpGuide.Org.
https://www.helpguide.org/articles/relationshi
ps-communication/effective-
communication.htm

Saunders, E.G. (2018, Dec. 19). *The 4 'Attachment Styles,'
and How They Sabotage Your Work-Life Balance*.
The New York Times.
https://www.nytimes.com/2018/12/19/smarte
r-living/attachment-styles-work-life-
balance.html

Smith, M., Robinson, L., & Segal, J. (2019, March 20).
Anxiety Disorders and Anxiety Attacks.
HelpGuide.Org.
https://www.helpguide.org/articles/anxiety/an
xiety-disorders-and-anxiety-attacks.htm

Steber, C. (2017, August 16). *13 Subtle Signs Your Partner
Is Unhappy In Your Relationship, Even Though
Things Have Seemed Great*. Bustle.
https://www.bustle.com/p/13-subtle-signs-
your-partner-is-unhappy-in-your-relationship-
even-though-things-have-seemed-great-76656

The Attachment Project. (2020, July 2). *Attachment Styles and Their Roles in Relationships*. The Attachment Project. https://www.attachmentproject.com/blog/four-attachment-styles/

Wignall, N. (2020, May 18). *Emotional Vulnerability: What It Is and Why It Matters*. Nick Wignall. https://nickwignall.com/emotional-vulnerability/

Wolff, C. (2018, January 17). *7 Unexpected, But Amazingly Effective Ways To Improve Your Relationship With Yourself*. Bustle. https://www.bustle.com/p/7-unexpected-but-amazingly-effective-ways-to-improve-your-relationship-with-yourself-7925162

Yandura, K. (2020, July 27). *The Difference Between Privacy and Secrecy*. Rewire. https://www.rewire.org/the-difference-between-privacy-and-secrecy/

www.ingramcontent.com/pod-product-compliance
Lightning Source LLC
Chambersburg PA
CBHW070119030426
42335CB00016B/2199